PEER PRESSURE

 Pulse

track: discipleship

Mike & Lesley Johnson

Kara Eckmann Powell
general editor

God's Word for a jr. high world

Gospel Light

Gospel Light is an evangelical Christian publisher dedicated to serving the local church. We believe God's vision for Gospel Light is to provide church leaders with biblical, user-friendly materials that will help them evangelize, disciple and minister to children, youth and families.

It is our prayer that this Gospel Light resource will help you discover biblical truth for your own life and help you minister to youth. May God richly bless you.

For a free catalog of resources from Gospel Light, please contact your Christian supplier or contact us at 1-800-4-GOSPEL *or* www.gospellight.com.

PUBLISHING STAFF
William T. Greig, Publisher
Dr. Elmer L. Towns, Senior Consulting Publisher
Pam Weston, Editor
Patti Pennington Virtue, Associate Editor
Jeff Kempton, Editorial Assistant
Kyle Duncan, Associate Publisher
Bayard Taylor, M.Div., Senior Editor, Biblical and Theological Issues
Dr. Gary S. Greig, Senior Advisor, Biblical and Theological Issues
Kevin Parks, Cover Designer
Rosanne Richardson, Cover Production
Debi Thayer, Designer
Virginia Bolenbaugh, Contributing Writer

ISBN 0-8307-2549-0
© 2001 Gospel Light
All rights reserved.
Printed in the U.S.A.

Peer Pressure

You may make copies of portions of this book with a clean conscience if:

- you (or someone in your organization) are the original purchaser;
- you are using the copies you make for a noncommercial purpose (such as teaching or promoting your ministry) within your church or organization;
- you follow the instructions provided in this book.

However, it is ILLEGAL for you to make copies if:

- you are using the material to promote, advertise or sell a product or service other than for ministry fund-raising;
- you are using the material in or on a product for sale;
- you or your organization are **not** the original purchaser of this book.

By following these guidelines you help us keep our products affordable.

Thank you,

Gospel Light

PRAISE FOR PULSE

There is a cry from this generation for Truth. **Pulse** curriculum targets this cry by leading teenagers to the Truth. How exciting it is to have a curriculum that gives the depth through Scripture and fun through involvement. —**Helen Musick**, Youth Specialties National Resource Team member, national speaker and author

The **Pulse** curriculum is truly "cross-cultural." Built on the solid foundation of an understanding of junior highers' unique developmental needs and rapidly changing culture, it affords teachers and youth workers the opportunity to communicate God's unchanging Word to kids growing up in a world that increasingly muffles and muddles the truth. —**Walt Mueller**, President, Center for Parent/Youth Understanding and author of *Understanding Today's Youth Culture*

The creators and writers of this curriculum know and love young teens, and that's what sets good junior high curriculum apart from the mediocre stuff! —**Mark Oestreicher**, Vice President of Ministry Resources, Youth Specialties

Great biblical material, creative interaction and USER-FRIENDLY! What more could you ask? This stuff will help you see your junior highers reach their potential as disciples of Christ! I highly recommend it! —**Ken Davis**, President, Dynamic Communications International and award-winning author and speaker

It's about time that curriculum produced for junior highers took them and their youth workers seriously. **Pulse** does it and does it very well! This curriculum knows junior highers and proves that teens changed by Christ who are equipped and empowered by His Church really can change their world! I am planning to recommend **Pulse** enthusiastically to all my youth worker friends. —**Rich Van Pelt**, Strategic Relationships Director, Compassion International, author, speaker and veteran youth worker

I found **Pulse** to be a stimulating, engaging and spiritually challenging curriculum for middle school students. Kara Powell has developed a rich resource that provides teachers with strong content to teach and creative options to help teachers meet the individual needs of their students. Recognizing that spiritual formation is not an end in itself, **Pulse** provides a strategy for evangelism in each lesson that empowers students to share the gospel with their peers. This is a curriculum that makes genuine connections with middle school students and the culture in which they must live out their faith every day. —**Mark W. Cannister, Ed.D.**, Chair, Department of Youth Ministries, Gordon College

Written by veteran junior high youth workers who know how to communicate so kids will get the message! Kara has given youth workers a fresh tool that's user-friendly and geared to make a lasting impact by addressing the foundational issues of Christianity that sometimes take a backseat to trendy topical studies. —**Paul Fleischmann**, Executive Director, National Network of Youth Ministries

This is serious curriculum for junior highers! Not only does it take the great themes of the Christian faith seriously, but it takes junior highers seriously, as well. Young adolescents have a tremendous capacity for learning about spiritual things and this curriculum makes it possible for them to learn all they can about the God of the Bible—who loves them and wants to involve them *now* in His Church. This is the best I've seen yet. —**Wayne Rice**, author and Junior High Ministry Director, Understanding Your Teenager seminars

Pulse
Peer Pressure

CONTENTSCONTENTSCONTENTSCONTENTSCONTENTS

Unit I: Outrageous Truths from the Old Testament

Unit II: New Insights from the New Testament

...You've Made the Right Choice in Choosing Pulse for Your Junior Highers

The Top Ten Reasons...

9. Junior highers need and deserve youth workers who are expert trainers and teachers of biblical truth.

Every book is pulsating with youth leader tips and a full-length youth worker article designed to infuse YOU with more passion and skill for your ministry to junior highers.

10. Junior highers equate who God is with what church is like. To them a boring youth ministry means a boring God.

Fun and variety are the twin threads that weave their way through this curriculum's every page.

8. Junior highers need ongoing reminders of the big idea of each session.

Wouldn't it be great if you could give your students devotionals every week to reinforce the learning goals of the session? Get this: YOU CAN because THIS CURRICULUM DOES.

7. Some of our world's most effective evangelists are junior highers.

Every session, and we mean EVERY session, concludes with an evangelism option that ties "the big idea" of the session to the big need to share Christ with others.

6. Since no two junior highers (or their leaders) look, think or act alike, no two junior high ministries look, think or act alike.

Each step comes with three options that you can cut and paste to create a session that works best for YOUR students and YOUR personality.

5. Junior highers' growing minds are ready for more than just fun and games with a little Scripture thrown in.

Scripture is the very skeleton of each session, giving it its shape, its form and its very life.

4. Junior highers learn best when they can see, taste, feel and experience the session.

This curriculum involves students in every step through active learning and games to prove to students that following Christ is the greatest adventure ever.

3. Tragically, most junior highers are underchallenged in their walks with Christ.

We've packed the final step of each session with three options that serve to move students a few steps forward in their walks with Christ.

2. Junior highers tend to understand the Bible in bits and pieces and miss the big picture of all that God has done for them.

This curriculum follows a strategic three-year plan that walks junior highers through the Bible, stopping at the most important points along the way.

1. Junior highers are moving through all sorts of changes—from getting a new body to getting a new locker.

We've designed a curriculum that revolves around one simple vision: moving God's Word into a junior high world.

Moving Through Pulse

Since **Pulse** is vibrating with so many different learning activities, this guide will help you pick and choose the best possible options for *your* students.

THE SESSIONS

The six sessions are split into two stand-alone units, so you can choose to teach either three or six sessions at a time. Each session is geared to be 45 to 90 minutes long and is comprised of the following four steps.

IT'S YOUR MOVE

A training article for you, the youth worker, to show you *why* and *how* to see students' worlds changed by Christ to change the world.

STEP 1 — MOVING IN

This first step helps students focus in on the theme of the lesson in a fun and engaging way through three options:

 MOVE IT—An active learning experience that may or may not involve all of your students.

 CHAT ROOM—Provocative, clear and simple questions to get your students thinking and chatting.

 FUN AND GAMES—Zany, creative and competitive games that may or may not involve all of your students.

STEP 2 — MOVING UP

The second step enables students to look up to God by relating the very words of Scripture to the session topic through three options:

 MOVE IT—An active learning experience that may or may not involve all of your students.

 CHAT ROOM—Provocative, clear and simple questions to get your students chatting about the Scripture lesson.

 PULSE POINTS—A message outline with simple points and meaningful illustrations to give students some massive truths about Scripture with hardly any preparation on your part.

 **STEP MOVING ON**

 **STEP MOVING OUT**

This step asks students to look inward and discover how God's Word connects with their own worlds through three options:

 CHAT ROOM—Provocative, clear and simple questions to get your students chatting.

 REAL LIFE—A case study about someone (usually a junior higher) who needs your students' help figuring out what to do.

 TOUGH QUESTIONS—Four to six mind-stretching questions that challenge students to a new level of depth and integration.

This final step leads students out into their world with specific challenges to apply at school, at home and with their friends through three options based on your students' growth potential:

 LIGHT THE FIRE—For junior highers who may or may not be Christians and need easily accessible application ideas.

 FIRED UP—For students who are definitely Christians and are ready for more intense application ideas.

 SPREAD THE FIRE—A special evangelism application idea for students with a passion to see others come to know Christ.

OTHER IMPORTANT MOVING PARTS

Bible Bonus Note

Extra information about the historical or cultural context of the Scripture passage to bring even more insight to your teaching.

Youth Leader Tip

Suggestions, options and/or other useful information to make your life easier or at least more interesting!

Devotions in Motion

WEEK FIVE: GRACE

Four devotionals for each session to keep the big idea moving through your junior highers' lives all week long.

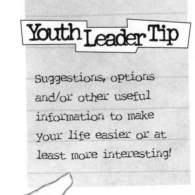

ON THE MOVE—An appealing, easy-to-read handout you can give your junior highers to make sure they understand that God's opinion is the *only* opinion that matters!

Peer Pressure

LEADER'SARTICLELEADER'SARTICLELEADER'SARTICLE

It's Your Move

God Is the Majority

Imagine standing shoulder to shoulder with eight others in front of a classroom of peers. You've been told you're there for a psychological experiment in visual judgement. You are shown two white cards: one contains a single dark, vertical line; the other has three vertical lines of various lengths. Your job? Choose the line on the second card that is the same length as the line on the first card. You think to yourself, No sweat, this is easy. It's line C. However, the six people who answer ahead of you choose line B. Now the pressure is on. Do you go along with the majority and choose line B, even when you are pretty confident it's line C, or do you stand up for your own minority opinion?

If you're like the college students who were originally involved in this well-known experiment conducted by S.E. Asch, you'll go along with the crowd one-third of the time. What you *don't* realize is that the previous six who have answered before you have all been instructed ahead of time to lie and choose an incorrect answer. What you *do* realize is that if you answer based on your own convictions, you'll be the only one saying line C, and you wouldn't want to be in that position, would you?

Now rewind in your memory to what you were like as a junior higher. You're not always as sure about what the right thing is, and even if you are, you certainly don't want to be the only one doing it.

We've carefully designed this book around three basic principles to help your junior highers know what the right thing to do is, and then stand up and do it.

10   Leader's Article

The Power of One

Here's a true/false statement: It takes a rare junior higher to stand up to the pressures to cheat, swear, become physically intimate, experiment with drugs and alcohol, or talk back to his or her parents.

Actually, it's a trick question. On the surface, the question is true, but maybe a truer statement would be: It takes a junior higher *connected to a rare God* to stand up to the pressures that bear down upon them. Your students will find it extremely difficult to muster their own strength to say no, when everyone around them is saying "yes." Apart from God, that is. (And even with God, it's not always easy!)

Perhaps you've heard the expression: "God plus one equals a majority." Actually, that's quite heretical. With or without anybody else, God is a majority. Period. In this book, we have tried to give your students all sorts of ideas to build their relationship with God so that they can become more aware of what it means to be on God's side.

The Power of a Few

Too many junior highers feel alone in their struggles with peer pressure. Sure, they hear that junior highers in general struggle with doing the right thing, but that's too abstract. They need time to hear about Suzie's struggles with cheating, Max's difficulties in knowing how to respond to the crude jokes he hears in P.E. and Jordan's confusion about how much he should be kissing his new girlfriend, especially since she seems to want to do it a lot.

Please, please, please take advantage of the small group options in these lessons so students can wrestle together with what it means to obey God in an ungodly world, until they eventually—hopefully—pin it down.

The Power of Many

Sure, it's been done before, but there is something empowering about being surrounded by a group of peers who stand, raise their arms or come forward together as a sign of their commitment to be kind to the less popular kids at school, to avoid pornography on the Internet or to share their faith even when it's difficult. Because of the powerful influence of *positive* peer pressure, we've given you all sorts of closing, rousing, group-bonding acts of commitment to help you form a group of young believers who, though limping at times, march forward together!

—Kara Eckmann Powell

Dedication

To our children: Abigail, Tristan and Elsbeth, who have given us a whole new perspective on youth work.

Contributor

Virginia (Gina) Bolenbaugh, author of the student devotionals, graduated from Seattle Pacific University in 1997 with a Religious Studies degree and completed her M.Div. at Fuller Theological Seminary in June 2000. Gina has worked with junior highers for many years and has recently followed her former junior highers into high school, serving as the Freshman Class Leader at Lake Avenue Church in Pasadena, California. She and her husband live in Pasadena.

The Big Idea

Standing firm under small pressures gives us the ability to stand firm under the big ones.

Session Aims

In this session you will guide students to:

- Learn that success is found in daily small things—not just in big things;
- Feel the importance of obeying God's Word in small ways in their everyday lives;
- Identify specific small areas where they need to stand against peer pressure this week.

The Biggest Verse

"Whoever can be trusted with very little can also be trusted with much, and whoever is dishonest with very little will also be dishonest with much." Luke 16:10

Other Important Verses

1 Samuel 16:7; Daniel 1:1-21; 3:1-30; Zechariah 4:10; Luke 19:11-27; 1 Peter 2:11,12

Little Things Make a Big Difference

STEP

MOVING IN

This step helps students begin to understand the significance that small things have in our spiritual lives.

Option 1  Move It

You'll need Chairs.

Greet students and ask them to arrange the chairs in a circle. Explain that they're going to play a game of Boppity-Bop-Bop-Bop. (That name should get their attention, don't you think?)

> **Note:** If your group is larger than 20, have students form two circles.

Here's how to play: You're It and your goal is to trick a student into taking your place. You're going to start saying the phrase "boppity-bop-bop-bop" by saying "boppity." You'll choose whether to say the whole phrase or just the first word and the student you point to has to figure out whether you're going to finish the phrase or not. If he or she thinks you're going to say the whole phrase, it's up to him or her to finish it before you can. If he or she thinks you're going to stop after the first word he or she must remain silent. If the student does not finish the phrase before you or if he or she mutters a word when you stop at the first "boppity," he or she is It! Play several rounds; then quickly comment about how people got better at the game the longer they played (this will relate to later parts of the session).

Explain: **We're starting a new series today on peer pressure. We'll see how the more you practice standing firm against peer pressure, the better at resisting it you'll become.**

Option 2  Chat Room

You'll need A white board, a dry-erase marker, a large serving tray, frosting (ready-made is fine) and homemade cupcakes (see next page).

Ahead of time, use the directions below to prepare two batches of cupcakes (get one or more of your students to help you if you can), but *leave out* the baking powder in one of the batches. The batch missing this small but vital ingredient will be very flat (which should make it fairly easy to keep the batches separated) and not quite as tasty!

4 tbsp. butter	1 cup flour
1/2 cup sugar	1 tsp. baking powder
1 egg	1/3 cup milk
1/2 tsp. vanilla	cupcake papers

Preheat oven to 350 degrees. Cream butter and sugar. Add vanilla and beat in eggs, mixing thoroughly. In a separate bowl, mix flour and baking powder (except in second batch, where you will skip the baking powder). Gently mix flour mixture into butter mixture. Add milk and mix. Put cupcake papers into muffin tin. Fill each cup two-thirds with batter. Bake for 15-20 minutes. Take them out of the muffin tins to cool, and then frost as desired. Makes about 6 cupcakes.

Greet students and bring out the tray of cupcakes without pointing out why some are flatter than others. If you have brave students, invite them to taste one cupcake from each batch; then write out the ingredients as listed above on the white board. Ask:

What's the difference between the two batches of cupcakes? One is flat and tastes kind of funny.

Explain that the difference between them is that one batch is missing an ingredient from the recipe. Ask if anyone can guess what the ingredient is and allow time for responses. Tell students the correct answer; then discuss:

How can such a small ingredient make such a big difference in a recipe? The baking powder has the most impact, even though it's one of the smallest amounts needed for the recipe.

Can you think of any other examples where what seems to be a small ingredient or part is vital for the whole thing to work? Parts in a car engine, a member of a sports team, the heart in the human body, the ripcord on a parachute, etc.

Transition by explaining: **We're starting a new series today on peer pressure and as we'll see, the small decisions we make when we're around others can have a big impact on our lives—and theirs.**

NOTES

Option 3  Fun and Games

You'll need An adult volunteer to referee, candy for prizes and one small unbreakable object for every student, something that can be passed from one person to another during the game.

Greet students and have them form a circle. Distribute an object to each student and instruct students to begin passing objects to their right when you give the signal. If an object is dropped, the student who dropped it will be escorted out of the circle by the referee, but the object will continue to be passed around. **Note:** You can make the game even livelier by yelling out "Reverse direction!" periodically so that players must pass objects the opposite way (and drop them in the process!).

Eventually, the objects being passed around will far outnumber the students still in the game. Signal to stop when two players are left; award them the candy prizes and explain: **As we start a new series on peer pressure today, we'll see that the better we get at standing firm against smaller waves of pressure, the better we'll be at standing firm against the bigger tidal waves that are sure to come.**

STEP MOVING UP

This step shows students that obeying God in small things is no small thing.

Option 1  Move It

You'll need Your Bible, a container of yellow or gold play dough for every three to four students and props for the characters from Daniel 3:1-30 (a horn for the herald to blow, ropes for the soldiers to tie up Shadrach, Meshach and Abednego, a halo for the fourth man in the furnace, etc.).

Divide students into small groups of three to four and distribute a container of play dough to each group. Inform students that they have one minute to create a sculpture of one person in their group. Give the signal to begin and call time after two minutes. Ask each group to show its sculpture and declare a winner. (You could award all of the play dough to the winning team, but remember: these *are* junior highers and you might wind up with it all over the meeting room!)

Place the winning statue on a chair or table at the front of the room and inform students that they're going to act out a Bible story. Assign the role of Nebuchadnezzar to the student whose likeness was sculpted and the roles of the Chaldeans, or officials, to the remaining students in the winning group. Ask for six additional volunteers and assign the following roles: Shadrach, Meshach, Abednego, the herald, two soldiers and the fourth man in the furnace. The rest of the group will play the people who fall down and worship the statue. You will narrate by reading Daniel 3:1-30 while the students act out the parts.

After the confusion (oops, we mean performance), discuss:

Why did Nebuchadnezzar set up the gold statue? He was arrogant, full of himself and he wanted to solidify his power as king.

Why did Shadrach, Meshach and Abednego refuse to bow down to the statue? They knew they should only worship God and that it was more important to obey God than to obey the king (see Daniel 3:12).

How did Nebuchadnezzar respond to their refusal to bow? He was pretty ticked off (see Daniel 3:13).

Were Shadrach, Meshach and Abednego 100 percent confident that God would save them from the fire in the furnace? Probably not, because they said that God *could* save them, but even if He didn't, they wouldn't bow down.

Does that mean they didn't have much faith? No, they had faith in God's ability to save them, but they also had faith that He would do what brought Him the most glory, which may or may not have been to save them.

Who was the fourth man walking in the furnace? Nebuchadnezzar called him a "son of the gods," but it's hard to say for sure who it was. Some Christian commentators have seen this fourth person as the preincarnate Jesus Christ, but he may just as possibly have been an angel sent to protect the men.

What effect did the courage of Shadrach, Meshach and Abednego have on the king? He came to endorse their God and granted them protection in his kingdom.

Read Daniel 1:1-21; then discuss: **How did the decision of Shadrach, Meshach and Abednego in this chapter prepare them for the furnace test that was to come?** It almost certainly prepared them to face this bigger challenge to their faith.

Option 2  Chat Room

You'll need Several Bibles, a TV, a VCR, the Veggie Tales video *Rack, Shack and Benny*, a white board and a dry-erase marker.

Ahead of time, cue the video approximately eight minutes from the beginning to the 10-minute scene in which Bob, Larry and Junior refuse to eat too much chocolate.

Distribute Bibles and ask several volunteers to take turns reading through Daniel 3:1-30; then explain that you're going to show a reenactment of the story, well, vegetable style! Show the video; then discuss:

What was Junior's (Shack's) reason for not participating in the chocolate feast? His mom told him too much candy was bad for him.

How did Junior convince Bob and Larry not to eat too many chocolate bunnies? By reminding them that they should obey their parents even when their parents aren't around.

Ask students to share examples of times when they've heard the phrase "Everybody's doing it" and how they responded when they heard it; then continue:

When Nebbie K. Nezzar asked Bob, Larry and Junior to bow down before the bunny, did you notice any difference in Bob and Larry's behavior? Bob and Larry didn't have to be convinced by Junior not to sing the song; they already knew what they believed and weren't willing to compromise.

How did the chocolate-eating experience prepare Bob, Larry and Junior for this new challenge? It gave them confidence to stand up for their beliefs and what their moms taught them, no matter what the cost.

What things does the video have in common with Daniel 3:1-30? Write responses on the white board (students should be able to come up with a long list).

Ask a volunteer to read Daniel 1:1-21; then discuss: **How did the decision of Shadrach, Meshach and Abednego in this chapter prepare them for the furnace test that was to come?** It almost certainly prepared them to face this bigger challenge to their faith.

Option 3  Pulse Points

You'll need Several Bibles, a large currency bill ($100) and several quarters. If it's tough to scrounge up a $100 bill on a youth worker's salary, write a check for that amount and make sure it gets ripped up afterward.

The Big Idea
Small decisions make a difference.

The Big Question
What kind of small decisions are important?

Explain: **Very often, people think bigger is better. For example, it used to be that you could buy a small soda in a convenience store or at the movies; now you can only buy soda in big cups. In fact, McDonald's doesn't even sell small sodas any more—the smallest size it sells is a "regular." Same thing with Starbuck's coffee—its small is called a "tall." Does that make sense?**

In God's eyes, however, size doesn't matter—not physical size or social status. Read Daniel 3:1-30 and explain that small things (a.k.a. unimportant things) are pretty important to God.

1. Small People
Compared to the king, Shadrach, Meshach and Abednego were pretty small and unimportant—yet their impact on the king was huge.

Invite an adult and one of the shorter students to come forward to act as visual aids as you illustrate that size, age or prestige makes little difference to God: **When Samuel**

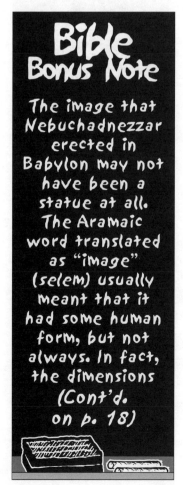

Bible Bonus Note
The image that Nebuchadnezzar erected in Babylon may not have been a statue at all. The Aramaic word translated as "image" (selem) usually meant that it had some human form, but not always. In fact, the dimensions (Cont'd. on p. 18)

was told to go and anoint David king over Israel, old Sammy was pretty impressed by the size of David's brothers (walk over to the adult). **But God said to him about David's brother Eliab, "Do not consider his appearance or his height, for I have rejected him. The LORD does not look at the things man looks at. Man looks at the outward appearance, but the LORD looks at the heart"** (1 Samuel 16:7). **To God, it's the condition of our hearts that matters, not the condition of our bodies; which means that no matter how young or small—no matter how** *insignificant* **we seem—God can still work through our decisions, even the small ones.**

> When an activity suggests bringing students forward based upon a certain physical characteristic, do not select students who may be adversely affected by having their differences pointed out.

2. Small Beginnings

Explain: **Sometimes we can become discouraged when we have to start small with something that we desperately want to be great at.** Share an example of an experience from your life where you had to learn a skill and were frustrated by not being good at it immediately; then continue: **Those times are sometimes the most important times, because often, that's when big things start.** Share the following illustration from a plaque marking the birthplace of Abraham Lincoln near Hodgenville, Kentucky:

"Any news down t' the village, Ezry?"

"Well, Squire McLains's gone t' Washington t' see Madison swore in, and ol' Spellman tells me this Bonaparte fella has captured most o' Spain. What's new out here, neighbor?"

"Nuthin', nuthin' a'tall, 'cept fer a new baby born t' Tom Lincoln's. Nothin' ever happens out here."

Ask: **Who were these men talking about?** Abraham Lincoln. Continue: **These guys thought that nothing important ever happened in their town, but one of the greatest American presidents was born there. It was a small beginning of a great life.**

Ask a volunteer to read Daniel 1:1-21; then point out:

When Shadrach, Meshach and Abednego refused to eat the meat that the king offered them, it probably seemed like a small thing; but it paved the way for the bigger challenges they would face later. In fact, if they hadn't resisted the pressure to eat the king's food, they probably wouldn't have been able to resist the pressure to bow down to the king's statue when their lives were at stake. The same thing is true for us—resisting the small pressures in our lives gives us the ability to resist bigger ones.

3. Small Actions

Explain: **For Shadrach, Meshach and Abednego it was the simpler action of refusing to eat the defiled meat that almost certainly prepared them for even bigger challenges to come. The same is true in your lives. It's those small actions that** will determine who you are and what you do when the big pressures come. It's how you respond when your classmates are giving the substitute teacher a hard time or what you say when friends are mocking the new kid's weird outfit—these small things prepare you for bigger challenges later on.

STEP 3
MOVING ON

This step helps students see that practice in their spiritual lives is just as important as it is in other areas of their lives.

Option 1 Chat Room

You'll need Unlined 3x5-inch index cards and pens or pencils.

Distribute index cards and pens or pencils and instruct students to draw a picture of themselves doing something that they are good at (i.e. playing an instrument, skateboarding, reading, etc.). Explain that it must be something they had to practice doing to become good at it. Allow three minutes or so; then ask several to share about what they drew. Discuss:

Is the thing you're good at easy or hard to do? It may be easy for the student but it still may be hard for other people to do.

Was it always hard (or easy)? Most things are hard to do when you first start doing them; they become easier with practice.

How did you become good at doing this? Practice; spending lots of time at it.

Did you enjoy all the times that you had to practice? Chances are that no one enjoys practicing something every single time they have to do it!

How does someone become a better Christian? Practice, practice, practice!

How can you practice being a Christian? By disciplining ourselves to do those little things we don't want to do such as reading the Bible, praying, fasting, tithing, etc.

How does practice relate to peer pressure? The more you're in the habit of saying no when everyone is saying, yes, (or vice versa), the better at it you'll become.

Option 2 Real Life

You'll need A thingymabopper and a whatchamacallit.

Share the following information about a famous golfer:

- His first name is Eldrick.
- His dad taught him every day about all aspects of the game—driving, chipping, putting.
- Knew the difference between a par 5, a par 4 and a par 3 at the age of 18 months.
- So talented, he demonstrated his golf skills on TV when only a toddler.
- Shot a 48 for nine holes at age three.
- Won his first Under-10 tournament at age four.
- Beat his dad for the first time on a par 3 course at age eight.
- Beat his dad no holds barred at age 11.
- Youngest player ever to win the U.S. Junior Amateur Championship (at 15) and won it two more times at 16 and 17.
- At age 18 he was the youngest player ever to win the U.S. Amateur Championship and won it two more times at 19 and 20.
- Youngest player ever to win The Masters (at 21) *and* set a Masters' record with a 12-stroke victory margin.
- Set a P.G.A. record, winning six tournaments in a row in the 1999-2000 season.
- His nickname? Tiger!

Discuss:

How did Tiger Woods become such an outstanding golfer? He had lots of raw talent, but it was his (and his father's) dedication to practice that made him great.

Do you think Tiger enjoyed all the days he went out to practice golf? Even though he loved his sport, there were probably times when he had to push himself to practice.

What would it take for you to become an excellent athlete or musician or salesperson or teacher? Dedication, practice, discipline.

If someone really wanted to be like Jesus, what would it take to become more like Him? Dedication, discipline, practice.

How does practice relate to peer pressure? The more you're in the habit of saying no when everyone is saying yes, (or for that matter, yes when everyone is saying no), the better at it you'll become.

You'll need Zees book and zeez questions.

1. **Do you have to be perfect to be a Christian?** 1 Peter 1:16 says, "For it is written: 'Be holy, because I am holy.'" God calls us to strive for perfection, but because of Christ's sacrifice, God will forgive us when we fall short of perfection. He doesn't want us to claim to be without sin, but rather to be quick to recognize when we sin and go to Him in repentance (see 1 John 1:8,9).

2. **If God is going to forgive me when I sin, why does it matter if I become a *good* Christian?** Being a Christian is about a lot more than just having our sins forgiven. Living in the kingdom of God means having abundant life now—a life that is full of joy and peace, in fellowship with God and other people. When we choose to sin, we miss out on that abundant life.

3. **OK, so if I practice and become a really good Christian, is my life going to be easier?** Unfortunately, no. Being a Christian—walking in Christ—can be a tough road to travel. There will be times when the *easiest* thing to do is to go against what we know God wants for us. We always have His promise to see us through those tough decisions and He has sent the Holy Spirit to guide us (see John 8:12,47; 16:13,14).

4. **Is it possible to be a good Christian without being seen as a goody-two-shoes?** To a certain extent, being a Christian will always be countercultural—Christians will never quite fit in with the world around them. But when we are truly trying to live a Christlike life, we will attract others to Christ. Some will accuse us of being goody-two-shoes, holier-than-thou and even persecute us because they are convicted by our behavior. Yet others *will* notice the difference and want to follow Jesus! (See 1 Peter 2:11,12)

5. **If God is all-powerful, why doesn't He just make it easier for us to resist temptation?** Consider the butterfly: it begins as a caterpillar, but it's not meant to stay that way. Before it can become what God designed it to become, it must work hard. First, it must build a cocoon for itself. After a period of time, the creature inside the cocoon is ready to come out, but breaking out of the cocoon is even harder than the original construction of it. As it struggles to break free of the cocoon, the creature becomes stronger and eventually a beautiful butterfly emerges. If the butterfly gets help in breaking out, its wings do not form properly so it can't fly. So it is with us—resisting temptation is how we work to become spiritually mature and going through tough times is how God molds us into the persons He's designed us to be.

STEP 4
MOVING OUT

This step helps students identify specific small areas in their lives where they need to obey.

Option 1  Light the Fire

You'll need Paper, copies of "Walk the Talk" (p. 22) and pens or pencils.

Distribute "Walk the Talk" and pens or pencils. Explain: **The items on this list are spiritual disciplines. They're spiritual because they help us grow closer to God, and disciplines because sometimes we have to push ourselves to do them.** Emphasize that these disciplines are not an end in themselves; they are ways to train us to become more like Christ. **Note:** The handout is not an exhaustive list of spiritual disciplines—it's simply a good foundation for students to build on.

Ask students to identify from the list one or two areas in their lives that they would like to change and then fill in the blanks for those areas. Allow a few minutes for students to complete the handout; then instruct them to write the name of a mature Christian they would like to have as a mentor for the next month—someone they feel comfortable discussing their need for spiritual discipline with. The mentors will keep in touch with the students, encouraging and holding them accountable for their spiritual discipline. Encourage students to think of someone besides you; however, offer yourself as an alternative mentor if students can't think of anyone else. Don't alienate students by discounting your own importance in their spiritual journey!

Invite anyone who would like to share what they wrote to do so; then take a few moments to ask students who they chose as their mentors for the week. Write down the mentors' names and offer to contact them with the requests if students would like for you to. Close in prayer, thanking God for providing ways for us to become stronger, better Christians and asking Him to help students to become spiritually disciplined in a way they can see during the next month.

Option 2  Fired Up

You'll need Copies of "Walk the Talk" (p. 22) and pens or pencils.

Follow the same basic directions in Option 1, but have the students fill out five or six areas in their lives where they would like to change. Try to set up a true mentoring relationship with the people the students indicated they would like to have coach them through the process.

Option 3  Spread the Fire

You'll need A copy of "Sharing Our Faith in Small Ways" (p. 24) for every three students and pens or pencils.

Divide students into groups of three and distribute one copy of "Sharing Our Faith in Small Ways" and pens or pencils to each group. Instruct students to work within their groups to come up with one small but difficult peer pressure situation involving friends in each of the four categories on the handout. Allow a few minutes for groups to work; then have the groups exchange papers and explain that students are going to come up with responses to the situations on the papers they exchanged.

Allow more time for students to respond; then have students return the handouts to their original groups. Invite volunteers to share the situations and the responses. Challenge students to commit to doing one or more of the items suggested. Close in prayer, thanking God for the opportunities He gives us to share our faith and asking Him to help students keep their commitments in the coming weeks.

NOTES

Walk the Talk

All good athletes know that they have to have a training regimen in order to keep their bodies in top shape to excel at their sport. We also need to have a training regimen in order to become more like Christ. We won't ever become better Christians just by sliding into discipleship; we must put ourselves into training. Look through the list below and choose specific areas where you want to go into training. Make sure you clarify how long you want to be committed to that training.

Prayer

Talking with God, setting aside specific times in our day to praise and thank Him, confessing our sins and bringing requests to Him

I commit to pray for _____ (how long) at _____ (what time) every day for the next _____.

Bible Study

Reading the Bible, reading devotionals or other books to help us understand the Bible, meditating (thinking) about what the Bible says

I commit to study the Bible for _____ (how long) at _____ (what time) every day for the next _____.

Solitude and Silence

Spending extended periods of time alone to listen to God

I commit to be in solitude and silence for _____ (how long) at _____ (what time) every day for the next _____.

Fasting

Going without food for a meal, a day or more than one day (clear this with your parents before you do this one), giving up other things (TV, movies, gum, sleeping in, etc.) for a period of time

I commit to fast from
(what) for _____ (how long)
_____ (how often) for the next
_____ .

Tithing

Giving money to the church or other Christian work

I commit to give _____ (how
much) to _____ (where)
(how often) for the next
_____ .

Humility

Not bragging about yourself, but considering others better than yourself

One way that I will practice humility is to
_____ for the next
_____ .

Service

Serving others through acts of kindness or mercy

One way that I will serve others will be to
_____ for the next
_____ .

Someone who can coach me through this and show me what to do, both by example and encouragement, is _____ .

Sharing Our Faith
in Small Ways

Here are four different places where junior highers can face peer pressure. Write a small area of temptation in each situation. For example, you might write "My friends make fun of Coach behind her back" in the class section or "My best friend is really disrespectful to his mom when I'm over there" in the weekend section.

In class

At lunch

After school

Weekends/free time

Devotions in Motion

DAY 1

QUICK QUESTIONS

Hey, head over to 1 Peter 5:6-11.

God Says

How much would you pay to be the strongest person at your school? Probably a lot, especially if you're a guy who wants to impress that new girl in your math class. Well, if you want to get real strength, check out 1 Peter 5:6-11.

In verses 6 through 9 each verse has one command (something that we should do) and a reason why we should obey that command. Fill in the following two columns (the first one is done for you):

COMMAND	WHY?
6: Humble yourselves	God will lift you up
7:	
8:	
9:	

What does verse 10 say is the ultimate result of obeying these commands?

I Do

Which of the verses do you find most helpful when you think about your struggle to stand under peer pressure? Why? Memorize that verse! Like right now!

FOLD HERE --

DAY 4

QUICK QUESTIONS

Check out Acts 15:36-40.

God Says

What happens when we fail? What happens when pressure comes and we give in to the pressure instead of doing what is right?

The good news is that everyone fails. Even the early followers of Jesus gave in to pressure at times! According to this passage from Acts, why didn't Paul want to take John Mark with him on his journey?

☐ He thought he dressed like a geek.

☐ His luggage didn't match.

☐ He had wimped out and deserted them before.

☐ His name was too confusing.

Later though, Scripture shows us that John Mark regained Paul's trust (see Colossians 4:10), and he even became an important part of Paul's ministry (see 2 Timothy 4:11).

I Do

Have you ever given into temptations or fallen under pressure? Who hasn't! The good news is that when we fail, God wants to restore us, or bring us back into a place of strength under pressure! Take a moment and ask God for His forgiveness during a time that you failed.

Is there someone else you need to apologize to? Or maybe someone else needs to know you forgive them. Remember the example of John Mark and Paul as you try to live your life standing firm under pressure.

FAST FACTS

Find Ecclesiastes 1:2,3. If you're a little lost, it comes after Psalms and Proverbs.

God Says

We all want to do big and important things, don't we? Really, who wants to do things that don't seem important? Like making your bed or setting the table or doing homework.

We'd rather do the big and important things that get others' attention and make a difference in the world, right?

According to Ecclesiastes 1:2,3, what is our job as creatures made by God? Does this seem big and important to you?

I Do.

Write down five things that you will do this week that may not feel very important but that are important according to this verse.

FOLD HERE --

FAST FACTS

If you want to see how the Bible describes a TV show, flip on over to Proverbs 2:1 2-19.

God Says

TV makes dating and romance seem pretty easy. Guy meets girl. Guy falls in love with girl. Guy sleeps with girl. Guy and girl are happy.

But what TV doesn't show you is some of the consequences of guy-sleeps-with-girl. Things like disease, heartbreak and feelings of emptiness, self-doubt and betrayal. And that's because the guy and the girl don't follow the Bible's plan for dating. They give in to pressures, both their own desires and the messages of our culture, and plunge in too deeply.

I Do.

You may not be dating right now, but some day you probably will be. What kind of relationships do you want to have? What kind of pressures will you give in to? Which ones will you stand strongly against?

Ask God right now to give you strength so that all of your relationships, including those with the opposite gender, are just like He would want them to be.

Peer Pressure

The Big Idea

It's easier to resist peer pressure if you don't willingly put yourself in situations where you'll face it.

Session Aims

In this session you will guide students to:

- Learn how to discern which tempting situations to avoid;
- Feel brave enough to walk away from negative situations;
- Learn how to walk away from challenging negative peer pressure situations they're bound to face soon.

The Biggest Verse

"And though she spoke to Joseph day after day, he refused to go to bed with her or even be with her." Genesis 39:10

Other Important Verses

Genesis 39:1-23; 40—50; Joshua 1:6; Proverbs 1:10-16; 4:10-15; 5:8; 26:11; 1 Corinthians 6:18; 10:13; 1 Thessalonians 5:22-24; 1 Timothy 6:11; 2 Timothy 2:22

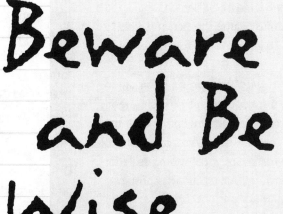

Beware and Be Wise

27

STEP

MOVING IN

This step will help students see that people sometimes put themselves in unhealthy—or even foolish—situations.

Option 1 Move It

You'll need A chair for every student and one for yourself.

Greet students and explain that they're going to play a memory game. Instruct them to move their chairs into a large circle (if the group is larger than 25 students, have them form more than one circle). Stand in the middle of the circle and explain the rules of the game: You're going to point at a student and name one of the original Three Stooges (Moe, Curly or Larry). If you name Moe, the student must state his or her name; if you name Larry, the student must name the person to his or her left; and if you name Curly, the student must name the person to his or her right. (Got it? Great, because we're totally confused now!)

If the student responds with the correct information before you can count to 10 as quickly as possible, he or she avoids having to switch seats with anyone—yet. If the student doesn't respond correctly before you can count to 10, he or she must trade seats with you. Trading seats for incorrect answers will ensure that students constantly have to remember new names!

After a few minutes of playing the game, stop and remind students that there were two Stooges that came after Curly: Shemp and Curly Joe. These names are now going to be added to the game. The same rules as before apply, but now when you name Shemp, the student you point to must name the person two seats to his or her left; if you name Curly Joe, the student must name the person two seats to his or her right. Whew!

Explain: **The Three Stooges were willing to do things that no one in their right mind would do. That's what made them so funny and popular. Unlike us, though, they were acting goofy because that was their profession. Sometimes we find ourselves in circumstances in real life where we do things we normally** wouldn't do. Oftentimes, those circumstances revolve around a group of people who are doing something that tempts us to go along with the crowd. Today we're going to look at some of the choices we make and the situations where we're more likely to do things we normally wouldn't.

Option 2 Chat Room

You'll need Dis book, see?

Greet students and share the following stories about some pretty foolish people:

> ⚠ CAUTION
>
> The stories in this option illustrate human foolishness. Gospel Light in no way endorses the beliefs represented on the Darwin Awards website, nor do we recommend accessing of the website by your students. Exercise discretion in giving out the website address.

- **Jumping Jack Cash**
(March 2000, Arizona) The Grand Canyon in Arizona is cordoned off by a fence around the more treacherous overlooks, to prevent unsteady sightseers from tottering into its depths. Some of these overlooks have small towering plateaus a short distance from the fence. Tourists toss coins onto the plateaus, like dry wishing wells. Quite a few coins pile up on the surfaces, while others fall to the valley floor far below. One entrepreneur climbed over the fence with a bag, and leapt to one of the precarious, coin-covered perches. He filled the bag with booty, then tried to leap back to the fence with the coins. But the heavy bag affected his jump, and several tourists were treated to a view of his plunge to the bottom of the Grand Canyon. He did not survive to harvest the piles of coins that had suffered his same fate.[1]

- **Dead Spitter**
(July 1999, Alabama) A 25-year-old soldier died of injuries sustained from a 3-story fall, precipitated by his attempt to spit farther than his buddy. His plan was to hurl himself towards a metal guardrail while letting his saliva build up in his mouth, in order to add momentum to his saliva. In a tragic miscalculation, his

momentum carried him right over the railing, which he caught hold of for a few moments before his grip slipped, sending him plummeting 24 feet to the concrete below.[2]

Discuss:

What made these people do such foolish things? Alcohol, greed, competitiveness, pride, etc.

What's the most foolish thing you've ever done? Remember, be prepared to answer first!

Do you think people are basically smart or foolish? Why?

Explain: **As we'll see today, lots of times we're more likely to do foolish things because we put ourselves in foolish situations. We're going to learn some great ideas about how to steer clear of trouble and avoid doing things we'll later regret.**

Option 3
Fun and Games

You'll need Two folding tables, four broiler pans (or heavy-duty cookie sheets), a stopwatch (or a watch with a seconds indicator), lots of cotton balls, some tissues or napkins for cleaning up, a jar of petroleum jelly and a prize for the winning team.

Ahead of time, set up the tables at opposite ends of the room and fill two of the broiler pans with cotton balls. Set the pans with the cotton balls on one table and the empty pans on the other.

Greet students and divide them into six teams. Ask each team to select a team representative to come forward. Once all six reps have come forward, explain that the teams are going to compete to see who can get the most cotton balls from one end of the room to the other. Yes, of course there's a catch: Contestants cannot use any body part except their noses to pick up and move the cotton balls!

Have two of the team reps step up to begin the game. Assign each rep one of the empty pans at the other end of the room; then smear petroleum jelly on their noses and signal the start. Allow exactly three minutes; then stop the game, count the cotton balls transferred by each team and set up for the next two team reps. Continue this until all six reps have competed. Announce the winning team's total; award that team its prizes.

Transition to the next step by asking the team reps if they felt foolish trying to move the cotton balls with petroleum jelly all over their noses. Explain: **We all put ourselves in foolish situations once in a while. Sometimes that's OK, but sometimes it can be really dangerous—especially when it comes to giving in to peer pressure or temptation. Right now we're going to find out that it's best to stay away from tempting situations when we can.**

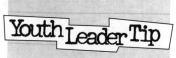

Junior highers love to play and watch games. Create a more exciting atmosphere and fill in the rare times when the audience is quiet during activities by playing some contemporary music. (Music can be used as the signal to start and end a game too.)

NOTES

STEP 2 — MOVING UP

This step helps students see that it is usually better to avoid temptation rather than fight it.

Option 1  Move It

You'll need Three prizes (gift certificates for ice cream, pizza or the next junior high event) and a watch with a seconds indicator.

Ask for one someone (the Tempter) who thinks he or she can get anyone to laugh and then ask for three Temptees who think that no one can get them to laugh. Explain that they will be playing "Go Ahead, Make Me Smile." The Tempter will be given 30 seconds to make each of the Temptees smile. Give a prize to the Tempter if he/she is successful in making someone smile or to the Temptees who are able to resist the urge to smile.

Transition: **Genesis 39 tells about a more serious temptation.** Briefly familiarize students with the betrayal of Joseph by his brothers that eventually led to Joseph's predicament with Potiphar's wife. Explain: **Imagine being Joseph. You've been sold by your brothers and now you serve an Egyptian master. Yet Genesis 39:2-6 repeatedly mentions how God was with Joseph. What does that tell you about God?** Allow for responses; then continue: **It might surprise you to find out that God is always with us, even when our circumstances seem to be going down the tubes.** Discuss:

Why wouldn't Joseph give in to Potiphar's wife? Because he knew that it would be a sin against God and against his boss.

What was Joseph's strategy to resist the pressure placed upon him by Potiphar's wife? He refused to even be near her (see Genesis 39:10).

Was it a good strategy? It worked as long as he wasn't near her.

Why did Potiphar's wife claim that Joseph attacked her? She was probably embarrassed and angered by his rebuff and decided to get revenge on Joseph for refusing her.

Explain: **Joseph was no fool. He knew that the closer he got to the fiery temptation of Potiphar's wife, the more likely he was to get burned by it. Although he ended up in jail anyway, it was his refusal to give in to the temptation to sin that eventually led to God opening doors for him to leave the jail and serve the pharaoh in ways that saved not only Egypt, but also much of Israel, including his own family** (see Genesis 40-50). **God honored Joseph's obedience to Him—maybe not in Joseph's preferred time, but in God's own perfect timing.**

Option 2  Chat Room

You'll need Several Bibles.

Ask students to share what their favorite food is; then ask if any of them have ever tried to give up their favorite food due to fasting, allergies or a diet. Allow for responses; then share the following story:

> **Kyle decided he wanted to lose some weight, so he made up his mind to go on a diet. The first day was really hard, especially during lunchtime when it seemed that everyone was enjoying huge sandwiches, chips and cookies—and all Kyle had was a plain salad.**
>
> **One afternoon, two days into his diet, Kyle got on his skateboard and skated his way over to the mall right past the ice cream parlor. Ooh, it smelled so good! He stopped, turned around, marched right in and ordered a banana split. The clerk brought the banana split to Kyle's table, and Kyle picked up the spoon and . . .**

Ask: **What do you think happened next? Did Kyle eat the ice cream or stick to his diet?** Allow for responses; then explain: **It was a really bad idea for Kyle to go into the ice cream parlor; it was probably not even a good idea for him to skate by the ice cream parlor so that he would be tempted to go in. If he really wanted to stick to his diet, he would have been better off to be aware of the temptation and avoid it.**

Discuss:

Some people are literally addicted to food. What other things can people be addicted to? Alcohol, work, gambling, TV, video games, sex, etc.

How can an addict kick his or her habit? Stay away from situations that would tempt him or her; get help from other people to not give in.

Distribute Bibles and ask a volunteer to read Proverbs 26:11. Explain: **Pretty gross, isn't it? It's true, though—someone who's addicted to something will have a really hard time staying away from his or her addiction.** Ask another volunteer to read 1 Thessalonians 5:22-24. Explain: **Instead of putting ourselves in situations** where we might be tempted, we should avoid them and turn our focus to God and His promise to be with us and help us resist the temptation to sin.

Option 3  Pulse Points

You'll need Several copies of the Good Book (no, not this one; although it is a good book, it's not *the* Good Book!).

The Big Idea

If we make smart decisions, we can avoid a lot of tempting situations.

The Big Question

What kinds of decisions should we be making to avoid tempting situations in the first place?

Distribute Bibles and ask several volunteers to take turns reading through Genesis 39:1-23. (You can decide where one student stops and another starts.) Explain that Joseph was a pretty smart guy. He knew that temptation was a hard thing to face. We don't know what Potiphar's wife looked like, but it had to be pretty tempting to have a woman throwing herself at him like that. There are two lessons we can get from the well-built and handsome Joseph (see Genesis 39:6).

1. Stay away from situations where peer pressure is a problem.

Ask if anyone has ever been to the Grand Canyon (or a similar canyon). Instruct students to close their eyes and imagine the following scenario:

> **You're on a tour of the Grand Canyon. It's so beautiful you can't believe your eyes. Your tour guide calls your attention to a cliff that drops half a mile straight down. She walks up to the guardrail and says, "This spot has absolutely the most beautiful view of the Grand Canyon. But to really get the full effect, you can't stay behind the guardrail." You're shocked as you find her climbing up and standing on the guardrail** (pause here for emphasis)! **Trying hard not to fall off, she says, "Everybody! Climb up here with me; it's great!"**

Explain: **If you have a death wish, you might join your tour guide up there on that guardrail a half mile above the ground. Most people, though, would decline. "That's OK, I'll pass. It looks just fine to me from here!" As strange as this story might sound, that's exactly what many people do with temptation; they allow themselves to be placed in situations where there's peer pressure to drink, smoke, have sex, steal or a whole host of other things.**

Joseph wouldn't stand up on the guardrail. In fact, he stayed way back from it by refusing to even be around Potiphar's wife. Joseph knew to stay away from pressure when he could.

2. Run away from peer pressure.

Share the following story:

> When Justin Armour was a rookie wide receiver with the Buffalo Bills, some veteran teammates invited him to a pre-season party. Justin went—and couldn't believe what he saw: Gorgeous women everywhere, offering free sex to any of the guys who wanted it.
>
> "It was the most eye-opening experience I've ever had," Justin says. "I had heard about things like this, but I was so naive. I got out of there as fast as I could!"
>
> As a single Christian guy, Justin had committed to saving sex for marriage. To do so, he knew he had to run from temptation.
>
> "I'd rather not have my mind polluted by those things. Once you've been in a couple [of] situations where's there's temptation, you learn how to avoid them and you don't go back."[3]

Continue: **Justin, like Joseph, knew to run away from temptation when it came pounding at his door. The great thing that Justin learned was that after you've run away from temptation a few times, you also learn how to avoid those situations in the future.**

Transition to the next step by explaining: **Instead of putting ourselves in foolish situations, it is usually best for us to simply avoid these negative peer pressures. But how do we know which ones we should avoid? This next step will help us figure out which situations in our lives we need to stay away from.**

STEP 3 MOVING ON

This step helps students discern which situations in their lives they should avoid.

Option 1 Chat Room

You'll need Two large bags of M&Ms (or a similar candy).

Divide students into groups of 8 to 10 and distribute 10 pieces of candy to each student. No eating the candy yet! Explain that groups are going to play "I Never." Here's how to play: **In each group, students will take turns saying something they've never done or some place they have never been (e.g., "I've never shaved my legs" or "I've never been to Florida"). Anyone in the group who has done that thing or been to that place must give one piece of candy to the student who hasn't.**

Allow several minutes for students to play; then regroup and discuss: **When someone has done something, he or she has gained experience. Is it better at your school to be experienced or inexperienced?** (Get ready—here come the giggles and answers about sex. Be prepared to keep the situation under control.)

In what situations would it be good to be able to say "I never did that"? Drinking, drugs, sex, stealing, etc.

How can we know which situations we should avoid? The Bible gives guidelines; parents, teachers, and other authority figures set rules to follow and advise us; more mature Christians can give good advice; seeing how certain behaviors destroy lives.

NOTES

Option 2  Real Life

You'll need A white board and a dry-erase marker.

Share the following case study:

> Ashley was 14 years old. One night at youth group, the youth pastor talked about God's plan that sex should be saved for marriage. She made a commitment that night to stay pure until her wedding night.
>
> Since Ashley's boyfriend, Nate, was 16 and wasn't a churchgoer, Ashley's parents weren't thrilled with their relationship. Because they trusted Ashley, they gave in and allowed her to see Nate—but only if they went out with a group of people.
>
> One Friday night Ashley and Nate made arrangements to meet at the movies with a group of friends. Nate's parents had let him borrow the car, and after the movie, Nate invited Ashley to go cruising. Her parents were expecting her to go out for pizza with the group after the movie, but she agreed to go with Nate anyway, reasoning that they would wind up at the pizza parlor after they drove around a little.
>
> Nate drove around and they eventually wound up in the park. Nate turned off the car and leaned over to kiss Ashley. He whispered, "Why don't we get in the back seat where we'll be more comfortable?"

Divide students into groups of five to seven and instruct the groups to discuss what Ashley should do. Allow three to five minutes for group discussion; then regroup and ask groups to share the advice they came up with. Discuss:

Nate was the one putting the pressure on Ashley, but what mistakes did Ashley make in this situation? She was wrong to go cruising with Nate when she knew her parents expected her to stay with the group; she was wrong to disobey her parents. You might point out that her first mistake might have been dating a non-Christian in the first place.

Draw three columns on the white board and ask students to come up with a list of similar peer pressure situations. (Examples might include: going to a party where people are drinking, hanging around with people who shoplift, getting involved in a gang, etc.) Write their answers in the left column.

Label the other two columns "OK" and "Not OK." Have students vote with a show of hands whether or not it's OK for a Christian to be in each situation and tally up the votes in each column. Ask students to defend their votes in each situation. Explain that Christians are not safe from temptation or peer pressure just because they hang out only with other Christians. What's important is to think about the situations we place ourselves in and be aware of our vulnerability to temptations.

Option 3  Tough Questions

You'll need Just these here questions.

1. **Is it OK for Christians to hang out with non-Christians?** Jesus Himself didn't always hang out with believers—in fact, He purposely sought those He could save. You must be discerning in your Christian walk. You can influence some nonbelievers and plant the seeds of salvation, but there are those whose behavior is tempting to you. It's a good idea to seek the advice of more mature Christians (such as a youth leader!) who can help you figure out who you should and shouldn't hang around with.

2. **What if your parents tell you not to hang around certain people?** God has put parents in the position to guide their children. Oftentimes, parents can see bad situations where you can't. You should always obey your parents, especially when it comes to the company you keep!

3. **Isn't the Holy Spirit supposed to give us the strength to stand up under any temptation?** The Bible does say that God will not allow us to be tempted beyond what we can bear and will provide a way out so we can stand up under it (see 1 Corinthians 10:13). But the Bible doesn't say that we should go looking for trouble and test God! In fact, 1 Corinthians was a letter

Paul wrote to people in a city known for immorality. He wasn't saying to go out looking for trouble knowing God will give you a way out; he was saying that God will give you a way out if you find yourself in trouble.

STEP 4
MOVING OUT

This step helps students know how to walk away from negative peer pressure situations.

Option 1 — Light the Fire

You'll need Copies of "Role-Play" (p. 36).

Ahead of time, cut the handouts into individual role-play scenarios.

Explain: **Peer pressure situations almost always have "pressure lines"—things that people say to really put the pressure on. One of the best ways to walk away from these situations is to come up with a good response to the pressure line. For example, a pressure line might be, "Come on, everybody's doing it." Your response could be, "Not everybody's doing it, because I'm not!"**

Divide students into groups of three to five and give each group a different role-play scenario. Let groups know that they have two minutes to come up with a role-play that ends with the person who's being pressured responding with a counter to the pressure line and walking away without giving in to the pressure. (All students in each group must participate in the role play). Allow two minutes for preparation; then have groups take turns acting out their role-plays.

Close in prayer, thanking God for giving us the courage and strength to resist temptation and the discernment to recognize some risky situations. Ask Him to help students know just what to say in order to walk away from tempting peer pressure situations.

Option 2 — Fired Up

You'll need A TV, a VCR, the video *The Wizard of Oz,* copies of "Courage Medals" (p. 37) and pens or pencils. **Option:** Copy the handout onto cardstock.

Ahead of time, cue the video approximately 49 minutes from the opening graphic to the scene where Dorothy meets the Cowardly Lion. **Note:** You'll be showing two clips from the video—the first ends when the characters head down the Yellow Brick Road; the second begins another 37 minutes into the video (an hour and 31 minutes from the beginning) where the Wizard gives the Cowardly Lion a medal.

Also ahead of time, cut the handouts into individual medals.

Show both video clips; then explain: **When Dorothy, the Scarecrow, the Tin Man and the Cowardly Lion finally meet the Wizard, the Lion learns that he has always had courage; he just lacked a medal. Just like the Lion, you already have courage. You have the courage to walk away from negative peer pressure.**

Distribute medals and pens or pencils and invite students to draw a symbol or picture in the middle of their medals representing a negative peer pressure situation they might need the courage to walk away from. (For example, someone may draw a cigarette if he or she is being pressured to smoke or a test if he or she is being pressured to cheat.)

Ask volunteers to share what they've drawn. Give each one who shares a personal word of affirmation about how courageous he or she is. Encourage students to carry their medals with them this week to remind them to have the courage to avoid giving in to peer pressure.

NOTES

Option 3  Spread the Fire

You'll need Copies of "Role-Play" (p. 36).

Ahead of time, cut the handouts into individual role-play scenarios.

Explain that most spiritual conversations start with springboard statements. These are statements that take whatever topic that's being discussed and turn it into a conversation about your faith. Explain: **Even negative peer pressure situations can turn into good opportunities to share your faith if you use the right springboard statements. Springboard statements use words like "God," "Jesus," "faith," "Bible" and "believe" to turn a conversation to spiritual things. For example, if someone is being pressured to do drugs, he or she could respond with "I don't need that—with God, I get high on life!"**

Divide students into groups of three to five and distribute one role-play scenario to each group. Instruct groups to come up with at least three springboard statements that could be used to start a spiritual conversation in the midst of peer pressure. Allow a few minutes for brainstorming; then regroup and have each group share its situation and springboard statements.

Close in prayer, thanking God for springboard statements that allow students to share the wonderful news of His love and asking that He would help students to have courage to speak the truth with their friends and family.

Notes
1. Bill Claxton, "Jumping Jack Cash." *The Darwin Awards*, March 2000.
   http://www.darwinawards.com/ (no access date).
2. Curtis Salisbury, "Dead Spitter," *The Darwin Awards*, July 1999.
   http://www.darwinawards.com/ (no access date).
3. Mark Moring, ed., *Men of Integrity*, Vol. 1, no. 1.

> **Youth Leader Tip**
>
> Never underestimate the insecurity of junior high students! Despite all their big talk and bravado, they are often still scared children on the inside. Because of this, they feed off of positive affirmation from us *older* folks. Look for ways to verbally build them up in whatever ways you can. The results will be amazing.

NOTES

Role-Play

Role-Play 1

You're at a friend's house on a Friday night. Your friend's older brother and his friends come in with some beer. They offer some to you, saying, "Come on, try it. It'll make you loosen up a little and have more fun."

How do you respond to this pressure line?

Role-Play 2

You and your friends are at a convenience store after school. Your friends come up with a plan for someone to distract the clerk so that everyone else can steal stuff. "Oh, come on," they plead with you. "That's why the prices are so high; they expect us to steal things. Besides, it's not like it's a car or something."

How do you respond to this pressure line?

ROLE-PLAY 3

A really popular guy in class whispers for you to show him your answers to the big test. "I'm too busy to study," he whispers. "I'll study next time. Be a pal!"

How do you respond to this pressure line?

Role-Play 4

You're at your friend's house when she gets a phone call from some good-looking guy who's at a home alone. He's got a couple of friends over and invites you and your friend too. Your friend wants to go, but you told your parents you'd be at your friend's house all evening. "Let's go for a little while," she says. "Your folks won't even know we left."

How do you respond to this pressure line?

Courage Medals

Devotions in Motion

WEEK TWO: BEWARE AND BE WISE

DAY 1

FAST FACTS

Walk on over to Proverbs 4:25-27.

God Says

Joey is confused: In this proverb, is God actually telling us not to go hiking in the mountains or walking along the beach because we should only make level paths for our feet and take ways that are firm? He continues, "I mean how can I ever get anywhere if I can't turn right or left?"

"No, no, no," you begin trying to calm poor Joey down. This proverb isn't about actually walking down the street. It is about the choices we make in life. God loves us and wants us to stay away from bad situations. God wants us to stay safe, so He uses the picture of walking to help us understand that. I mean, when you walk on ground that isn't even, after a while you'll probably fall and hurt yourself. In the same way, if we don't make wise choices, we can get hurt—or well end up going the wrong direction and getting lost!"

Joey is so lucky to have a wise friend like you!

I Do

Rewrite this proverb in a way that Joey (and maybe some of your friends) can understand it better.

How can you walk straight ahead today?

FOLD HERE

DAY 4

FAST FACTS

Check out John 6:14,15—like pronto.

God Says

Isn't that interesting? Even Jesus had to avoid certain situations at times! The funny thing is that some situations look good on the outside but aren't so good when you look deeper into them. These are some of the hardest situations to avoid! For instance, don't you want to ask Jesus what is wrong with being a king? Well, we know that Jesus will reign on Earth as King someday—but it will happen when God the Father puts Jesus on the throne and not because people tried to force it.

I Do

Have you ever been in this kind of situation, one that looks good at first but really isn't good? Think about it. What was so good about that situation at first? Maybe it was the attraction of a certain guy or girl or maybe the acceptance of your friends.

Whatever it was, when and how did you discover that the situation that looked good really wasn't so good?

Ask God to give you wisdom and insight so that in future situations you will not jump into things that only look good on the outside but are not good when you look deeper into them.

QUICK QUESTIONS

DAY 2

Run over to Jonah 1:1-5,12-17; 2:10 and 3:1-3.

God Says

Wow. There's a lot to the story of Jonah, but from the small sections that you have just read, what was Jonah trying to do? He was trying to run away from God! What two things did God send to let Jonah know that He was going the wrong way?

- ☐ An e-mail and a balloon-a-gram
- ☐ A storm and a huge fish
- ☐ Charlie's Angels and James Bond
- ☐ The school cafeteria lady and the school security cop

I Do.

God still works today! In the past, you have probably gotten into situations that were bad. Can you think of ways that God tried to redirect you? (Hopefully not through a large fish but maybe through friends or Bible verses or songs that came to your mind at just the right moment.)

What ways might you expect God to warn you when you're tempted to do something you shouldn't do?

Spend some time thanking God for working on you!

FOLD HERE -

QUICK QUESTIONS

DAY 3

Dig into Mark 6:21-28.

God Says

OK, gross! And bad! Now, before King Herod did the awful thing you just read about, he felt distressed (v. 26). In other words, he didn't actually want to follow through on what was asked of him—but he did it anyway! Why did he do it?

- ☐ He didn't want to look lame in front of his guests.
- ☐ He wanted to gross out his guests.
- ☐ His guests were getting bored and he wanted to liven up his party.

I Do.

The things we say or promise to do can get us into trouble! Herod chose to do the wrong thing because he swore a promise in front of a crowd of important people he wanted to impress.

In the same way, we sometimes talk our way into bad situations—especially when we are talking to people we are trying to impress.

What are two ways you can keep yourself from talking your way into bad situations? (It could be a single word you say to yourself to hold you back, such as "Herod," or it could be a friend who will warn you?) Write those two ways down!

Peer Pressure

The Big Idea

Negative peer pressure loses its punch if we know who to listen to and who to ignore.

Session Aims

In this session you will guide students to:

*   Learn to discern who they should listen to;
*   Feel a sense of unity with other students in establishing high standards of behavior;
*   Covenant as a group to encourage godly behavior in the future.

The Biggest Verse

"But Rehoboam rejected the advice the elders gave him and consulted the young men who had grown up with him and were serving him."
1 Kings 12:8

Other Important Verses

1 Kings 11:9-13; 12:1-20;
Proverbs 2:3-6; 3:5,6; Acts 15:32;
Hebrews 3:12,13; 10:24; Titus 2:6,7;
James 1:5

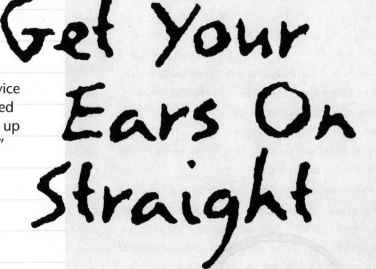

Get Your Ears On Straight

STEP
MOVING IN

This step helps students see that groups can either lift people up or tear them down.

Option 1  Move It

You'll need A large meeting space—ideally multiple rooms (or outside spaces) with small hiding places.

Greet students and explain that you're going to start this session with a variation of Hide and Seek called "Sardines." It's actually the reverse of the original game; in Sardines one person hides and the rest seek! When a seeker finds the person hiding, instead of yelling out the discovery, the seeker hides with him or her in that same space. This continues, with the seekers becoming hiders until a large group of people is crammed inside a small hiding place.

Play a few rounds, and then bring everyone back together and explain: **This game is interesting because it sometimes takes a long time to find the first person, but as the number of people hiding in one area grows, it becomes pretty obvious where they are hiding. Groups are noticeable, and the bigger the group, the more noticeable it becomes.**

A person can be involved in many different types of groups. Sometimes these groups are encouraging, but sometimes they push us toward things we know we shouldn't do. Today we're going to look at which groups and which people we should listen to.

Option 2  Chat Room

You'll need Several stale and several fresh donuts (make sure you know which ones are stale, but no one else can tell), a knife, a plate and an adult volunteer to supervise.

Ahead of time, cut the donuts into bite-sized pieces and arrange them on the plate.

Also ahead of time, call five students from your group and let them know you'll be choosing them as volunteers

during this step. Their job is to pretend that the stale donuts are the best tasting ones.

Greet students and ask: **Who likes donuts?** As you're blinded by a sea of raised hands, select eight volunteers (the five you called and three more). Pretend to randomly choose the three new volunteers to go out of the room with the adult volunteer. Explain to the rest of the group that the five remaining volunteers were preselected and that you're going to show students the power of group pressure.

Call one of the three volunteers back into the room and let him or her know that you're going to conduct a donut taste test. Invite all six of the volunteers in the room to taste the two types of donuts, making sure to allow the five preselected ones to go first. (The new one will be pressured to go along with the other five.) Allow for his or her vote; then explain the truth about the test and ask him or her to play along as you call another volunteer in. Repeat the process for the seventh and eighth taste testers; then interview the three volunteers who had to undergo the pressure:

How did it feel to have everyone else saying that the stale donuts tasted better when you totally disagreed?

Did the pressure change your answer at all?

Were you tempted to give in?

Discuss with the entire group: **Is it harder to resist peer pressure that's coming from one person or pressure that's coming from a group of people?**

Explain: **Group peer pressure is typically harder to resist. Groups of people have a lot of power—in fact, they have so much power that we've got to make sure we know which ones to listen to.**

Option 3  Fun and Games

You'll need Prizes for the winning team.

Greet students and divide them into equal groups of 8 to 10. (If you have fewer than 16 students, give a 30-second time limit for completing the task.) Explain that they're going to play a game called " Out of the Pits". In round one, each person in a group will take turns lying flat on the floor. The remaining team members will work together to lift their teammate waist high; then set him or her back gently on the floor. The first team to successfully lift each of its member wins that round.

Round two is the similar to round one, except that once someone has been lifted, he or she may not help lift others. Allow 30 seconds to develop a strategy; then play round two. Award prizes to the team that successfully lifts the most members and discuss:

How did it feel being lifted by your teammates?

How did round one compare with round two? Fewer lifters made it more difficult.

Explain: **This game is kind of like our lives as Christians. The more people we have lifting us up, the easier it can be. When we work together to lift up all members of our group instead of tearing them down, we'll find that the Christian life becomes a lot easier for all of us. Now let's take a look at an ancient king who got involved with the wrong group.**

STEP 2 — MOVING UP

This step helps young people discern which group of people they should listen to for advice and guidance.

Option 1 — Move It

You'll need Several Bibles, two adult volunteers, a bag of potato chips, two blindfolds and a prize for the winning team (small bags of chips, maybe?).

Divide students into two teams and ask for one volunteer from each team. Inform the volunteers that their task is to cross the room without stepping on any of the chips you will spread across the floor. Ah, that's too easy. Let's blindfold them! They must lift their feet with each step—no shuffling across to move chips out of the way.

Teammates will call out instructions to guide their team rep across the room while calling out false instructions to sabotage the other team rep. No one except the two team reps is allowed to step inside the area where the chips are at any time. Blindfold the team reps and then spread several chips on the floor in their pathways. Give the signal to begin and ask the adult volunteers to help you keep track of the number of times the reps step on chips; then declare a winner after they both make it across.

Award the prize to the winning team; then ask the two who crossed how hard it was to discern which voices to listen to. Allow for responses and distribute Bibles. Set the stage by explaining that after King David died, his son Solomon became king. After Solomon died, his son Rehoboam became king of Israel. Ask five volunteers to read through 1 Kings 12:1-20 (each reading four verses); then explain: **Rehoboam's problem here was similar to this game: He couldn't figure out which voices to listen to. His father, Solomon, had taxed the people heavily and required his followers to serve as laborers and military soldiers** (see 1 Kings 12:4). Discuss:

Youth Leader Tip

According to research, junior highers would rather ask their parents for advice than anyone else. It's only when their parents aren't available that they ask others. In today's world, peers have become influential by default. For too many kids, parents are no longer there for them—they're either non-existent or too busy. And the extended family? It's all but vanished for today's youth. The bottom line is that today's junior highers are more influenced by peers and the media than ever before because those are the influences most consistent in their lives. (Adapted from Wayne Rice, Junior High Ministry [Grand Rapids, MI: Zondervan, 1998], p.94.)

What kind of advice did Rehoboam get from the elders? To be a servant to his people.

Why do you think he rejected their advice? He probably viewed servanthood as weakness and wanted to be absolutely powerful.

Who did he turn to? His peers—people who were about his age.

What was their counsel? To put an even heavier burden on the people.

Read 1 Kings 11:9-13. Discuss: **What word of the Lord was being fulfilled in 1 Kings 12:15?** The prophecy that the house of David would be punished for Solomon's idolatry and breach of the covenant.

What happened to Rehoboam? He was forced to flee and he lost most of the kingdom to Jeroboam.

Explain: **It's true that older people who have more life experience tend to give better advice than younger people. This is especially true for older Christians who've had more time to grow in their relationship with the Lord. Christians who are more mature, both in age and in spiritual maturity, are usually good people to rely on for sound advice. If we pay attention to people who are wise, we're bound to make better choices. If not, we'll end up destroyed or wind up hurting people around us—just like Rehoboam.**

Option 2 — Chat Room

You'll need A white board, a dry-erase marker, two pieces of paper and two pens or pencils.

Divide students into two teams and distribute paper and a pen or pencil to each team. Explain that the teams are going to list as many TV or radio talk shows as they can in one minute. Give the signal to begin and have them stop writing after one minute.

Have each team read its list and use the white board to record what they came up with (use a column for each team). After you've listed each team's answers, cross out all duplicate talk shows; then add up the number of names each team listed that the other did not. Award 100 points for each unique answer and declare the winning team. Discuss:

What's the most ridiculous thing you've ever seen or heard on a talk show?

Do people give good advice on talk shows?

Would you follow the advice given by someone on a talk show?

Share the background info from Step 2, Option 1; then tell the story of King Rehoboam found in 1 Kings 12. Explain that Rehoboam's situation was similar to that of people who go on talk shows; he received opposing advice from different sources. He chose to follow what turned out to be the harmful advice.

> **Optional:** Use the discussion questions in this step's Option 1 in addition to the following questions to help students dive even further into the passage.

Discuss:

Who do you know that you can always count on for good advice?

Why would you choose this person to give you advice?

What keeps you from going to these people all the time? Like Rehoboam, we listen to people who tell us what we want to hear when we would be better off listening to people who tell us the hard truth; people who have the experience to know what they're talking about.

Explain: **Sometimes, we don't think about the advice we get when the pressure's on. When people are pressuring us to do something we know we shouldn't do, we tend to listen to their advice instead. Now we're going to look at how who we listen to determines how we respond in peer pressure situations.**

Option 3 — Pulse Points

You'll need A TV, a VCR, a video camera and a blank videotape. **Low-tech option:** Use an audiocassette recorder/player instead of video.

Ahead of time, video- or audiotape children's answers to the following question: "What do you need to remember when you're driving a car?"

Also ahead of time, video- or audiotape *adults'* answers to the same question.

The Big Idea

If we listen to the right people, we'll make better decisions.

The Big Question

What kind of people should we be listening to?

Use background information in Step 2, Option 1 to set the stage and then summarize the story of Rehoboam in 1 Kings 12. Explain: **Rehoboam made a bad decision because he listened to the wrong people. We learn a few things about the kind of people we should be listening to from Rehoboam's story.**

1. Listen to those who tell you the truth, not just those who say what you want to hear.

Explain: **Usually, when people like us need advice, where do they go? Ann Landers? Dr. Ruth? Dr. Laura? No, we usually go to our friends—and this can be a big mistake. While our friends can be a support to us when we have to make tough decisions, they often can't see the situation from all sides. They end up giving advice based more on what they think we want to hear, rather than on what's right.**

Illustrate by asking students to pair up and stand back-to-back. Instruct them to listen for your signal and change one thing about their appearance (glasses on upside down, shirt buttoned wrong, belt off, etc.). When you give the signal again, partners will turn to face each other and the partner who recognizes what's different on his or her partner first will move to the right side of the room; the other partner will sit out. Instruct students still in the game to pair off again and repeat the process of elimination until you have a winner.

Explain: **When something is out of place, or wrong with how you look, don't you want to know? When you have that piece of spinach stuck in your teeth or that hair sticking straight up, you want your friends to tell you the truth, right?** Of course! **King Rehoboam's friends decided not to tell him the truth. They flattered him by telling him that his little finger was thicker than his father's waist—a fancy way of saying that he was more important than his father, King Solomon. Were they telling him the truth? No. Isn't it interesting that most people know about King Solomon, but very few know about his son Rehoboam? Instead of going to people who will tell us what we want to hear, we should go to people who will tell us the truth and give us good advice.**

2. Listen to those who are experienced, not those who think they know the right answer.

Play the video (or audio) interviews and comment on the main difference in the advice people gave: the children (who had no experience) couldn't give real advice about driving but the adults (who were experienced) knew what they were talking about.

Transition to the next step: **Rehoboam heard from two groups, but he decided to listen to those who had less experience. We've probably all received advice from people who had no clue what we were going through or those who had never been in our situation. People often think they have good ideas on what to do, but unless they've been in the situation they're advising on, they really have no idea if their advice will work! The truth is that it's the people who've faced many difficult situations in their lives who can give the best advice.**

STEP 3 MOVING ON

This step helps students understand that choosing which group they listen to determines how they will face peer pressure situations.

Option 1 Chat Room

You'll need A TV, VCR and the video *Star Wars*.

Ahead of time, cue the video approximately one hour, 51 minutes from the opening graphic to the scene in which Luke Skywalker blows up the Death Star.

Play the video clip through the scene where Obi-Wan says, "The Force will always be with you" and then discuss:

Why did Luke put down the targeting scanner? Luke heard (or remembered) Obi-wan telling him to use the Force instead.

How do you think Luke would have handled the situation if he hadn't been trained by Obi-wan? He probably wouldn't have known what to do.

In the Star Wars universe, what does someone have to do to become a Jedi knight? Go through extensive training with another older and wiser Jedi.

When you face peer pressure, do you think about what your parents or other adults have taught you? Why or why not?

What percent of the time do you actually decide to do what you've been taught?

Name one situation where you should be living out what wise people have taught you instead of listening to the people who are pressuring you.

Transition: **We all need to remember what wiser, more experienced people have taught us, but we also need to be part of groups that encourage us and help us resist peer pressure. As we close, we're going to look at how the group we're in right now can be that kind of group.**

Option 2 — Real Life

You'll need Copies of "Dear Dr. Advice" (p. 49), paper and pens or pencils.

Ahead of time, cut the handout into individual letters.

Divide students into small groups of three to five and distribute one advice letter, paper and a pen or pencil to each group. Explain that students are writers for an advice chat-room for teens on the Internet called "Dear Dr. Advice." Groups should discuss possible responses to the letters they received.

Allow a few minutes for brainstorming; then ask each group to share its letter and advice with the whole group. Discuss the advice given; then explain: **As part of a responsible group of caring friends, we need to give each other good, solid advice that encourages one another to make good decisions and resist negative peer pressure.**

Option 3 — Tough Questions

You'll need The truth, and nothing but the truth, so help you God (and boy, do we mean that literally!)

1. **How do I know which older people are wise?** A couple of ways. First, you can ask for their advice in a small situation and see if you think it's good, sound advice. You can also ask several people for advice and compare what they say to see which seems the most wise and appropriate to what you're going through. We can always ask God to help us understand what is the best advice (see Proverbs 2:3-6; 3:5,6; James 1:5).

2. **Does this mean I should *never* listen to the advice of my friends?** Sometimes friends give good advice, but you shouldn't rely on them as your primary source of guidance. If a friend gives you advice that seems questionable to you, make sure you run it by someone else you trust.

3. **What if I don't have anybody to rely on for sound advice?** You can ask someone in the church (a certain youth worker, maybe?) or a friend's parents. It's not a little thing, either, that God is *always* ready to listen when we're confused and in need of counsel. Ask Him to bring someone into your life who you can trust to give sound advice. God Himself will advise you if you take the time to build your relationship with Him, spending time in prayer and reading the Bible.

4. **If I ask two people to help me figure out what to do and they give me different advice, what should I do?** First, ask God and read His Word to find out what He thinks about your situation; then ask a few other people you respect for their advice. Prayerfully accept the advice that you feel God wants you to follow.

Transition to the next step by explaining: **Whether or not you have people to go to for good advice, guidance and encouragement, you can help this youth group become a place in which you can find that kind of help. Let's look at how we can help our group become an encouraging place for junior highers to come to for advice.**

STEP 4
MOVING OUT

This step helps the group establish itself as an environment where godly behavior is encouraged.

Option 1  Light the Fire

You'll need Just a group of junior highers (and you probably wouldn't have read this far if you didn't already have that!).

Ask for an adventurous volunteer to stand outside the room. Once he or she is outside the room, explain that the rest of the group is going to vote on something in the room that the volunteer must touch when he or she comes back in. Students will clap and cheer as the volunteer gets closer to the object and boo as he or she gets further away from it. Bring the volunteer back into the room and tell him or her what's going on (but not what the chosen item was, of course!). If you have time, you can do this with one or two other students.

After playing a couple of rounds, explain: **This is exactly what this group should be for everyone in this room: support. As we get closer to doing the things God wants us to do, we should cheer for each other. If we start doing stuff that we shouldn't do and give in to negative peer pressure, we should gently correct each other—the key word here is gently. No booing, but we need to lovingly confront someone who is on the wrong path! Let's close by praying that we would be supportive and encouraging to one another.**

Option 2  Fired Up

You'll need Volunteers to share testimonies, room enough for each group of six to eight students to meet without overhearing other groups and one copy of "Accountability Group Questions" (p. 50) and an adult to act as facilitator for each group.

Ahead of time, arrange for volunteers to share their experiences facing peer pressure. Ideally, the testimonies should include having to make a hard decision in the midst of negative peer pressure and how positive peer encouragement helped in the midst of a tough situation.

Ask the volunteers to share their testimonies and be sure to highlight the difference between trying to stand under pressure alone versus handling it with a friend. Explain that one of the goals of this session is to establish accountability groups: **Accountability is just a big word for helping someone really live as a follower of Jesus. In order for accountability groups to work, you must trust one another. Even more important, you must be trustworthy. In order to ensure this, the accountability groups will have two rules:**

1. **Total Confidentiality—Everything said within an accountability group stays within the group—anything said should never be shared with anyone outside of that group, not even with a member of another group.**
2. **Total Forgiveness—When a member of an accountability group confesses having done something wrong, other members in the group must be committed to completely forgiving that person and encouraging him or her to resist the temptation in the future. No one in an accountability group should *ever* be judgmental toward another member.**

Divide students into small accountability groups and assign each group an adult (or high school age) facilitator. Distribute "Accountability Group Questions" and send each group to a different area for privacy. Have students select some of the questions on the handout to discuss within their group. **Note:** It's important that the facilitator be a participant and answer the questions just like everyone else.

Allow several minutes for group discussion; then bring everyone back together as a whole group (have the small groups stay close, though) and establish a time that each group will meet once a week for the next month. A good time might be just before or just after your regular large group meeting. Have facilitators close the session by leading their accountability groups in prayer.

Note: After a month, meet with the facilitators to evaluate if the groups are meeting their purpose. If so, continue meeting; if not, have them work with you to modify or disband groups that aren't working out.

Option 3
Spread the Fire

You'll need Patience!

Ask for a volunteer who's pretty physical—but not violent—to come up and stand by you. Instruct the group to form a tight circle in another part of the room. When you give the signal, the volunteer should do everything he can to get inside the circle (give no instructions to the rest of the group). Give the signal and watch as students forming the circle do all they can to keep him out. Call a halt to the madness; then discuss:

Why was this person kept out of the circle? "Because you told us to!" should be the reply.

Did I specifically tell anyone not to let him into the circle? Well, no, not exactly.

Explain that the only instructions you gave were to the volunteer. He was to try to penetrate the circle, but you didn't say anything about keeping him out! Continue: **Many groups of friends are this way; somebody wants to become part of the group, but the group does all it can to exclude that person. Positive groups are open to new friends and encourage godly behavior. If you really want to bring your friends to Christ, you must constantly make sure that our group is friendly and inviting for new people to join.**

This may be a good time to have a frank discussion about how open the group is to new people. Ask students to think about how often they invite their non-Christian friends, and how comfortable they think their friends would be when visiting the group.

Close by having students form a circle and hold hands. Let go of the hand of the student to one side of you and explain that in breaking the circle this way, the group is symbolizing the openness of the group to new people. Have several students pray for their non-Christian friends. Close with a prayer of covenant for the group to always be open and inviting to newcomers.

NOTES

Dear Dr. Advice

Dear Dr. Advice,
People at school talk a lot about sex. They say that everybody is doing it—and that people who haven't done it yet are just babies. My youth pastor says it's not true that everybody is doing it and that even a lot of the people talking about it haven't done it. I'm not sure who I should believe. I don't want my friends to think I'm weird. Who should I listen to?

Dear Dr. Advice,
My mom and dad are going away for the weekend and my brother and I get to stay home alone. They say we can't have anyone over while they're gone, but what do they expect me to do—sit home alone the whole weekend? My friends said we should have a small party with just a few people over. What could it hurt to have just a couple of friends over? Aren't my parents being way overprotective and controlling?

Dear Dr. Advice,
Since school started again, I've been getting involved in a lot of partying. Most of the parties I go to have older kids who drink. I know it's against the law—and definitely against what my parents say—but everyone is doing it. I'm always hearing how alcohol would help me to relax and have even more fun. I'm not stupid enough to get in a car with someone who's been drinking, but why can't I have a little at a party?

Dear Dr. Advice,
I'm 12 and I started middle school this year. I've made new friends and they make fun of my best friend from elementary school. We don't hang out much now that we're in middle school, but I don't tease him like my new friends. But I don't defend him, either. I like my new friends and I like my old friend. What should I do?

Accountability Group Questions

Select five or six questions to discuss. Remember to keep everyone's answers confidential—don't share them with anyone outside your group.

- Have you spent time praying this week on a regular basis?
- How have you served other people this week?
- Do you treat your peers as people who are loved by God?
- What significant thing did you do for your family?
- What was your biggest disappointment? How did you decide to handle it?
- What was your biggest joy? Did you thank God?
- What do you see as your number one need for next week?
- Did you take time to show compassion for others in need?
- Did you control your tongue?
- Did you read God's Word this week?
- How have you been tempted this week? How did you respond?
- How has your relationship with Christ been changing—for good or bad?
- Did you worship in church this week?
- Have you shared your faith this week? How?
- What are you wrestling with in your thought life?
- What have you done for someone else this week?
- Are the *visible* you and the *real* you the same person?
- Have you lied in your answers to any of these questions?

Devotions in Motion

WEEK THREE: GET YOUR EARS ON STRAIGHT

DAY 1

QUICK QUESTIONS

Jog over To Proverbs 4:14,15.

God Says

Here we are, walking again!

What does it mean To seT foot on The path of The wicked or walk in The way of evil men? What does God want us To do instead of walking with Them or being like Them?

- ☐ Hightail it out of There.
- ☐ Fall down and play dead.
- ☐ Stop, drop and roll.
- ☐ Shake, raTTle and roll.

I Do

Think of your friends. You probably wouldn't call Them evil exactly, but maybe you have a few friends who do sTuff ThaT isn'T so great. When you hang out with Them, you end up doing ThaT wrong sTuff Too. Pray for your friends and also ask God To show you how To go This way and To give you The strength To do it! And just maybe, your friends will follow you on The righT paTh!

FOLD HERE -

DAY 4

FAST FACTS

Blow over To Hebrews 10:23-25.

God Says

A liTTle poem for you:

Spunky The racehorse had losT her spunk
(IT seems she had fallen inTo some sort of a funk).
So Amber The rider
SaT down asTride her
And sTuck her spurs in Spunky's rump.

When we spur each other on we are helping each other To conTinue living in a way ThaT will please God. God wanTs us To know ThaT it is so imporTanT To have friends To geT TogeTher with for The purpose of encouraging and spurring each other on!

I Do

Who are your Two closesT ChrisTian friends? What can you do in The nexT Three days To help Them please God?

QUICK QUESTIONS

Check out Proverbs 13:20 and 1 Corinthians 15:33.

God Says

Have you ever heard the saying "One bad apple spoils the whole bunch"? Well, the Bible says something very similar in the verses you just read. What do these verses mean? Imagine that you are explaining these verses to an alien from Pluto. How would you restate these verses so that your new friend from Pluto could understand them?

I Do

Think about the people you hang out with. Are they good or bad influences on you?

Who do you know who helps you stay on track with God in the way you talk, think and act?

What about you—how do you influence your friends? Spend some time praying that God will show you how to be a good influence in your circle of friends today or even that He will give you the strength to find new friends if all of yours constantly pull you down.

FOLD HERE --

FAST FACTS

Breeze over to Hebrews 3:12-14.

God Says

We all need encouragement, right? But what does that word mean anyway? It means to give courage to. There are lots of things we need courage to do. For instance, you may need courage to speak to that cute girl or guy. Or you might need courage to try out for that sports team or that part in the play. Even more than those things, though, it takes courage to live your life for Jesus.

I Do

In the past week or two, has someone given you courage to follow Jesus? Who gave you that encouragement and when? Write your encourager a thank-you note!

Also, write down four ways that you can give courage to a friend to live for Jesus, and make sure you do it this week!

SESSIONFOURSESSIONFOURSESSIONFOURSESSIONFOUR

The Big Idea

Knowing and applying Scripture can help us resist negative peer pressure.

Session Aims

In this session you will guide students to:

- Understand how knowing the Bible can help them resist peer pressure;
- Feel convicted to memorize Scripture to help in tempting situations;
- Commit to applying Scripture to different temptations they face this week.

The Biggest Verse

"Jesus answered, 'It is written: "Man does not live on bread alone, but on every word that comes from the mouth of God."'" Matthew 4:4

Other Important Verses

Deuteronomy 11:18; Psalm 119:9-11; Matthew 4:1-11; Luke 4:1-13; Colossians 3:16; 1 Timothy 6:10; 2 Timothy 3:16; Hebrews 4:12; James 1:22

STEP
MOVING IN

This step helps students examine how much they know about the Bible.

Option 1  Move It

You'll need Chairs and a rolled-up newspaper.

Ahead of time, arrange the chairs in a circle. (Form more than one circle if your group is larger than 20 students and arrange for an adult volunteer to help with each additional circle of students.)

> Note: This option works best if students are familiar with biblical characters.

Greet students and instruct them to take a seat; then ask them to select a character from the Bible (everyone must select a different character—no duplicates.) Stand in the middle of the circle and point to a student. He or she must say the name of his or her Bible character and the name of another character. The student whose character is named second must repeat his or her character's name *and* the name of another (but not the previous name) before you can bop him or her on the head with the newspaper!

After a few rounds, discuss:

What was David famous for? Killing Goliath, writing psalms, being king, etc.

What did he do well? He was a good shot! He was also a good leader of his people.

What did he do not so well? Leading his family, avoiding temptation, etc.

Explain: **Sometimes we look at people in the Bible as if they were fairy tale characters instead of real people who struggled with real-life pressures not all that different from what we deal with today. We can learn some valuable lessons from how they responded to the tough challenges they faced. As we'll see today, the more we understand the Bible and apply it to our lives, the better we'll be able to respond to temptations around us.**

Option 2  Chat Room

You'll need Paper, pens or pencils and candy prizes.

Greet students and explain that you are going to give them a quick Bible quiz, and anyone who gets the questions *all* right will win a prize. Instruct students to number their papers from one to six and then ask the following questions (don't give the answers!):

1. **Is the book of Hezekiah before or after the book of Psalms?** Neither, there is no book of Hezekiah in the Bible.
2. **Who in the Bible said, "Do to others as they do to you"? A) Moses; B) Jesus; C) Paul** No one. Jesus said, "Do to others what *you would have them* do to you" [Matthew 7:12, emphasis added].
3. **In what book of the Bible does it say, "Money is the root of all evil"? A) Deuteronomy; B) Matthew; C) 1 Timothy** No book. The Bible says, "*The love of* money is a root of all kinds of evil" [1 Timothy 6:10, emphasis added]. If someone gets picky and says that it technically does say "money is a root of all evil" within that phrase, give them credit for a right answer.
4. **Which of the Ten Commandments says, "Love your neighbor as yourself"? A) 2nd; B) 5th; C) 8th** None of the Ten Commandments. Jesus said this in Luke 10:27, quoting from Leviticus 19:18, which is not part of the Ten Commandments.
5. **In what book of the Bible does it say, "God helps those who help themselves"? A) Proverbs; B) Ecclesiastes; C) 1 Corinthians** None. That quote is attributed to Ben Franklin.
6. **What did Jesus turn stones into A) Bread; B) Fish; C) Water** Jesus never turned stones into anything. He was tempted by Satan to turn them into bread, but He didn't.

Share the correct answers and award a prize if anyone got them all right. If no one did, feel free to award prizes to the student(s) who got the most correct. (That is, unless you want to keep the candy for yourself. Hey, we don't get many perks in youth ministry, so we have to take them where we can find them.) Then discuss:

Do most people in your school know much about the Bible?

On a scale of 1 to 10, how would you rate your knowledge of the Bible?

On a scale of 1 to 10, how would you rate what you *want* your knowledge of the Bible to be? What kinds of things would you have to do to know more?

How would being more familiar with the Bible affect the way you respond to temptations?

Continue: **Knowing the Bible well is the first step but, as we'll see today, if we want to stand against peer pressure, we'll also have to apply it as well!**

Option 3  Fun and Games

You'll need The "Who Wants to Be a Bible-aire?" questions (p. 62), coins and a few dollar bills to award as prizes.

Ahead of time, you might want to make the questions into overhead transparencies or PowerPoint so everyone (including the contestant) can see them.

Greet students and explain that this game is modeled after *Who Wants to Be a Millionaire?* Start with a fastest-time round where several students compete to become the contestant. Whoever raises his or her hand first and then answers correctly gets to be the contestant.

Contestants will have three lifelines. They can 1) poll the audience (where you read each answer and have the audience either raise their hands or cheer for the answer they think is right); 2) 50/50 (where you remove two of the wrong answers) or 3) ask a friend (where the contestant has 60 seconds to ask a friend what he or she thinks is the right answer).

Here are the money values for each round: First Round: 1¢ (make a big deal about this); Second Round: 2¢; Third Round: 3¢; Fourth Round: 6¢; Fifth Round: 10¢; Sixth Round: 15¢; Seventh Round: 25¢; Eighth Round: 50¢; Ninth Round: 75¢; Tenth Round: $1.00.

Play all 10 rounds and then transition to the rest of the lesson by explaining: **Most people today don't know very much about the Bible. In fact, it's been said that half of all Americans cannot name Genesis as the first book of the Bible, and 14 percent think Joan of Arc was Noah's wife. It's too bad that people don't know more about the Bible, because I have found it to be a great book to base my life on. But it's not enough to just know about the Bible; we have to go deeper to really help us know what to do when we face tough questions or temptations.**

STEP 2 MOVING UP

This step helps students see the importance of memorizing Scripture in standing against peer pressure.

Option 1  Move It

You'll need Your Bible and a quick mind.

Have students stand and try to repeat everything that you say, exactly as you say it—even though it is very strange. If possible, have volunteers monitor whether students say everything properly or not. Anyone who misses must sit down. Start with the first item, then add one more each time (so the first time you will say, "One hen," the second time, "One hen, two ducks," and so on).

1. One hen
2. Two ducks
3. Three squawking geese
4. Four limerick oysters
5. Five porpulent porpoises
6. Six pairs of Dynal Virgil's tweezers
7. Seven thousand Macedonians in full battle array
8. Eight solid brass monkeys from the sacred, ancient crypts of Egypt
9. Nine sympathetic, apathetic, diabetic old men on roller skates with a marked propensity toward procrastination and sloth
10. Ten lyrical, spherical, diabolical denizens of the deep who stall around the corner of the quo on the quay of the quivy

Award a prize to the student(s) who gets the farthest. Share the importance of being able to memorize vital information (phone numbers, locker combinations, a speech for class, music). Then explain: **We all have to memorize things. Usually, we memorize things because it's necessary to have them right when we need them. Let's read a story about what Jesus memorized.** Read Matthew 4:4-11. Follow up the story by explaining: **The devil makes temptations attractive, just as he did in the first temptation by asking Jesus to turn stones into bread when Jesus was extremely hungry**

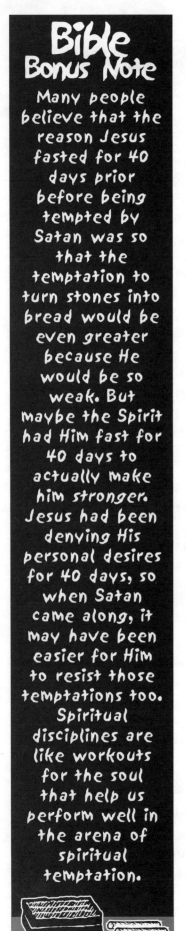

Bible Bonus Note

Many people believe that the reason Jesus fasted for 40 days prior before being tempted by Satan was so that the temptation to turn stones into bread would be even greater because He would be so weak. But maybe the Spirit had Him fast for 40 days to actually make him stronger. Jesus had been denying His personal desires for 40 days, so when Satan came along, it may have been easier for Him to resist those temptations too. Spiritual disciplines are like workouts for the soul that help us perform well in the arena of spiritual temptation.

after his 40-day fast. In the second temptation, the devil offered the world to Jesus through an easy path rather than through God's plan. In the third temptation, Satan tempted Jesus to test God's faithfulness and attract attention to Himself. In all three cases, Jesus had memorized Bible verses (see Deuteronomy 8:3; 6:13,16) so He had them when He needed them. Jesus was able to face every temptation the devil threw at Him because He had important verses memorized.

Option 2  Chat Room

You'll need A white board, a dry-erase marker and a picture of something that brings a good memory for you (a vacation, wedding, birthday, etc.). Also, if possible, ask students the week before to bring a picture of a good time in their lives. (It's a good idea to call them during the week to remind them.)

Display the photo and explain what's happening in the picture and why it's a good memory for you. If students have brought pictures, have them share why their pictures are good memories for them. Discuss:

Share your earliest memory.

Tell about a time when you had to memorize something and how you felt about it.

Memorizing things is easy/hard for me because . . .

What can you do to help you remember something more easily?

Is memorizing Bible verses important, or is it enough to just have a pretty close idea of what a Bible verse says?

After the discussion, have someone read the story of Jesus' temptation in Matthew 4:1-11; then summarize the contextual information included in the previous option. Discuss:

How did Jesus face Satan's temptations? He quoted Bible verses.

Can you think of a Bible verse that could help you stand up against a temptation? "Flee sexual immorality"; "Don't get drunk with wine"; etc. (Write suggestions on the white board as a visual reminder.)

Option 3  Pulse Points

You'll need Three Bibles of the same translation and a Band-Aid for each student.

The Big Idea
Studying the Bible can make a difference in how we respond to temptations.

The Big Question
How can the Bible make a difference in responding to peer pressure?

Introduce this talk by asking for three volunteers to help do a dramatic reading of Scripture: a narrator, Jesus and Satan. Have each volunteer read his or her respective lines from Matthew 4:1-11; then share some of the contextual information included in this step's Option 1.

Explain: **This is a really cool story because each time Satan tempted Jesus, Jesus answered by quoting a verse from the Bible. This passage tells three ways we can use the Bible to its full potential when we face temptations.**

1. We Need to Open the Bible.

A lot of Christians don't know much about the Bible, but the more we read it, the more we see how it applies to our lives. Distribute one Band-Aid per student. (**Note:** We are not saying that the Bible is like a spiritual Band-Aid; this is just an object lesson.) **All of us have used Band-Aids at one time or another. They are great for helping to heal cuts, scrapes, blisters, etc. But they don't do much good sitting in the package, right? You have to open it in order for it to do any good.** Invite them to open their Band-Aids, but not to take the paper off the sticky part yet. Continue: **The same thing is true for the Bible. Lots of people have Bibles, but most never open them. The Bible does us no good unless we open it to see what's inside.**

2. We Need to Memorize God's Word.

Explain: **It is not enough just to open the Bible; we need to memorize it to help it stick in our minds. Look at your Band-Aid. What's the gauze in the middle for?** The gauze helps protect and heal the cut. **The gauze would be worthless, though, without something to hold it on your skin. That's why Band-Aids have that sticky stuff; it helps the gauze stick to the skin. Memorizing verses is just like that sticky stuff; it helps the Bible verses stick in our heads. Jesus had memorized Scripture and pulled them out when He needed them.** Have them remove the paper from the sticky parts of the Band-Aid, but not stick it on their skin yet.

3. We Need to Apply Scripture.

Unless you actually take the Band-Aid and stick it to your skin, it is worthless. You might know the whole Bible and memorize lots of verses, but if you never apply it to your life, it won't help you at all. Encourage them to apply their Band-Aid somewhere on their skin where they can see it and leave it there for the rest of the session (actually, in true junior high fashion, you might want to have a contest to see who can keep theirs on the longest during the next week). **Jesus had memorized Scripture and was able to apply it when Satan tempted Him.**

NOTES

STEP 3 MOVING ON

This step helps students understand that they can trust the Bible to guide them when they're facing tough peer pressure.

Option 1 Chat Room

You'll need Copies of "Lost in the Translation" (p. 63).

> **Note:** Junior high students love chaos. Instead of passing out papers the way teachers do in school, just take the papers and throw them in the air to various parts of the room. Your students will generally make sure that each person gets one.

If you have had any experience trying to communicate with someone who doesn't speak English well, share a brief story about it. It doesn't have to be funny or profound, it's just important that it's *your* story. Then explain: **Sometimes, it's hard to translate things between different languages. Things sometimes get lost in the translation.** Distribute "Lost in the Translation" and have volunteers read some of the mistranslations aloud to the group. Then discuss:

What causes these translations to come out so badly? Words from one language don't mean exactly the same thing as words in another language; different people interpret words differently; the people who translated these things probably didn't know English very well.

How many languages was the Bible written in originally? Three: Hebrew, Greek and Aramaic.

How can we know that it was translated properly? The English translations were made by large teams of scholars who were fluent in the three languages; any mistranslation would probably be caught by one of the other translators; many believe the Holy Spirit not only inspired the writers of the Bible, but also guided the translators.

How does all of this make you feel about the Bible and its accuracy?

If you believe that the Bible is trustworthy, what difference would that make in the way you use it to stand against peer pressure? If we know something is true, that makes it a lot easier to consistently obey what it tells us to do and be like.

Option 2 Real Life

You'll need A model that you put together (or better yet, have a couple of students from your ministry help you put it together during the week before the meeting)—without using the instructions. Hopefully, it will be a mess, which is exactly the point.

Show the model and tell about your experience putting it together, making sure to highlight how difficult and frustrating it was to do without the instructions. Discuss:

What things do people do in which following instructions is important? School assignments, recipes, computer programs, crafts, etc.

Have you ever *not* followed the instructions in one of these areas? What happened? Briefly share about how you have decided to follow the principles found in the Bible as the instructions for your life. If you have a testimony about what your life was like before you followed biblical principles, briefly share it now.

How does following the Bible's instructions relate to peer pressure? The Bible gives us all sorts of principles, stories and examples that will help us figure out what to do when people are pressuring us to do something we shouldn't do.

Explain: **It's not always easy to follow what the Bible—the ultimate instruction manual—says about our lives. But think about it: God made us, and He knows what's best for us. If we ignore what He has to say to us, then we're going to end up just like this model—pretty messed up.**

NOTES

Option 3 — Tough Questions

You'll need Just these here questions.

> **Note:** A good resource for difficult questions is Josh McDowell, *The New Evidence That Demands a Verdict* (Nashville, TN: Thomas Nelson, 1999).

1. **How can we know the Bible is true?** 1) Because Jesus Christ, God's own Son and our Savior, had complete faith and confidence in the trustworthiness of God's Word (see Matthew 5:17-19). 2) We can know God's Word is true by putting it into practice and experiencing His promises. 3) We can examine the internal consistency of the Bible's message and the external consistency of history and archaeology. 4) We can look at the impact Jesus and the Bible have had on the world throughout history.

2. **How can we know the Bible is the same today as it was when it was first written?** As an ancient document, the Bible is better preserved than any other historical document. There are thousands and thousands of handwritten manuscripts of the Bible that still exist, while there are only very few copies of other ancient documents still around. Also, archaeological findings have confirmed many details of the stories of the Bible. In comparing ancient copies with today's copies there are only minimal differences between the old and the new versions. And yet these external proofs might be disputed by disbelievers, so once again we must trust in the reliability of God's Word as we put it into practice in our own lives and see the results in the lives of others.

3. **Doesn't the Bible contradict itself?** If you look at the Bible as a whole you will see that there is one central theme to the entire Book: God's desire to bring redemption and salvation to humanity. This unifying message is gradually unfolded throughout Scripture until the life, death and resurrection of Jesus Christ brings it all together. When we let the Bible as a whole speak for itself, these so-called contradictions evaporate.

4. **If the Bible was written in other languages, how can we know that our translation is really what God meant to say?** The English translations were made by large teams of scholars who were fluent in all the languages and these teams cross-checked one another's work to insure accuracy. A lot of research and study goes into the translation of the Bible into any language, often taking many years to accomplish. The Holy Spirit who inspired the writers of the Bible, also guides the translators today.

5. **Given how old the Bible is, how can it still be relevant to the peer pressures we face today?** Great question, but the answer is wrapped up in God Himself. God's been around for a *long* time—actually forever—He's just as relevant to us as He was to the very first humans. He doesn't change, and neither does the truth of His Word. When we understand its stories and principles, we can apply them to life in the 5th century, the 12th century or the 21st century.

STEP 4 — MOVING OUT

This step helps students memorize and apply the Bible to specific areas where they are tempted to give in to peer pressure.

Option 1 — Light the Fire

You'll need Several Bibles, a white board, a dry-erase marker, paper and pens or pencils.

Ahead of time, write the following list on the white board:

- Focusing on Physical Appearance: 1 Samuel 16:7; 1 Timothy 2:9,10; 1 Peter 3:1-7

- Cheating: Leviticus 6:1-5; 19:36; Proverbs 11:1; 1 Corinthians 6:7,8
- Drinking/Drugs: Proverbs 23:29-35; 31:4-7; Ephesians 5:18; 1 Peter 4:3,4
- Gossip: Exodus 23:1; Proverbs 25:18; 2 Thessalonians 3:11,12; Titus 3:1,2

Share the following story:

> Imagine you're just hanging out with friends, when all of a sudden the most beautiful girl (or the most handsome guy) in school walks right up to you. He/she says, "Hi. I've had my eye on you for a while, and I think you're cute. I want to get to know you better. I'd like you to come over and have dinner at my house tomorrow night. Here's a map to my house and the address. Come over at 6:00 P.M. Don't be late!"
>
> He/she then hands you a note and walks away, giving you a little wink over the shoulder. You open up the note, and it is the messiest thing you have ever seen! The handwriting is so bad you can't understand a word, much less where the streets are! Ask: **What would you do? Would you toss the note and skip the dinner date or would you do all you could to find out where the house is?** Allow for responses; then explain: **As strange as it may sound, many people approach the Bible in just the same way as the people who might just throw the note away. They honestly want to have a relationship with God, but sometimes the Bible just seems too hard to figure out. So they leave it on a shelf, and it does them no good whatsoever. The Bible isn't always easy to figure out, but the result is worth the search.**

Divide students into groups of four to six. Distribute Bibles, paper and pens or pencils; then explain that each of the topics on the board deals with a different peer pressure situation. Have each group choose one of the topics listed to research (more than one group can choose the same topic, but make sure all of the topics are represented) and look up the verses for their topic; then write down in one sentence what the Bible says about it. Have adult volunteers help groups that may have difficulty. After a few minutes, have groups share their results with the whole group.

Guide students in a time of silent prayer, confessing to God a peer pressure situation that they're tempted to give in to and asking God to help them live out what the Bible says.

Option 2 — Fired Up

You'll need Paper and pens or pencils.

Instruct students to form pairs. Explain as you distribute paper and a pen or pencil to each pair: **On this paper, write out a few sentences describing a really tough peer pressure situation that a Christian junior higher is likely to face at school.**

After a few minutes, have pairs switch papers. Explain: **Atheists are people who don't believe in God. Unfortunately, a lot of time even Christians act like atheists; we act like God isn't around to guide us and help us. Take a few minutes to discuss this situation with your partner and write down how an atheist would respond.**

After a few minutes, continue: **Hopefully those of us in this room will act differently. Why? Because we're trying to obey God's Word. Now take a few minutes to discuss and then write down how someone would act who believed the Bible was true and was committed to letting it affect their behavior.**

When the pairs are finished, ask a few to share their answers with the rest of the group. Close in prayer, asking God to help us all act like Jesus would want us to when we face tough peer pressure situations this week.

Option 3 — Spread the Fire

You'll need Copies of "Vital Verses" (p. 64).

Ahead of time, cut the verses apart and, if possible, laminate them.

Explain: **A vital part of sharing our faith is knowing Scripture verses that explain the gospel. In that way, we can use positive peer pressure to explain how much Jesus has done for us, and how much He offers our friends also. But often we don't have a Bible around when the opportunity arises to share our faith. That's why it is important to have these verses memorized, so that we can use them at any time.**

Distribute the "Vital Verses" cards. Have students pair up and memorize some of the verses by alternating words in the verse (one student says one word, the other student says the next).

Challenge students to carry their verses in their wallets, backpacks, etc. and pull them out during the week to practice memorizing them. Pray that students will have opportunities to use the verses during the week.

NOTES

Who Wants to Be a Bible-aire?

Fast Round Questions

1. Put these people in the order in which they appear in the Bible.
   a) Abraham; b) Jacob; c) Isaac; d) Joseph   (Answer: *a, c, b, d*)

2. Put these books of the Bible in order.
   a) Exodus; b) Leviticus; c) Genesis; d) Numbers   (Answer: *c, a, b, d*)

3. Put these books of the Bible in order.
   a) Romans; b) John; c) Acts; d) 1 Corinthians   (Answer: *b, c, a, d*)

Contestant Questions

Correct answers in *italics*.

1. What holiday celebrates Jesus' rising from the dead, so we who believe can do the same?
   a) Christmas; b) Valentines Day; c) Thanksgiving; *d) Easter*

2. How did Judas identify Jesus for the priests?
   a) Put his arm around him; *b) Kissed him*; c) Gave him his staff; d) Shook his hand

3. What is 1 Corinthians chapter 13 all about?
   a) Love; b) Sin; c) Peace; d) Satan

4. What did Jesus do in the Garden of Gethsemane?
   a) Worship; *b) Pray*; c) Hide; d) Sleep

5. What teenager was thrown into a pit by his brothers?
   a) Jacob; b) David; *c) Joseph*; d) Elijah

6. "He leads me in the paths of righteousness for his name's _____."
   a) Holiness; *b) Sake*; c) Jesus; d) Understanding

7. Where does the Bible say the final world war will take place?
   a) Jericho; b) Jerusalem; c) Babylon; *d) Armageddon*

8. Which biblical character lived the longest on earth?
   a) Noah; *b) Methuselah*; c) Abraham; d) Moses

9. What was the first plague on Egypt?
   a) Locusts/grasshoppers: b) Killing of all first-born; c) Day turned to night; *d) River turned to blood*

10. Which of the disciples was a tax collector?
    a) Mark; *b) Matthew*; c) Luke; d) John

11. Which is not a part of the Trinity?
    a) Father; b) Jesus; c) Holy Ghost; *d) Angel*

12. What was the job of Joseph, Mary's husband?
    a) Carpenter; b) Doctor: c) Innkeeper; d) Janitor

13. If Eve ate the forbidden fruit, the serpent said she would be like whom?
    a) Adam; *b) God*; c) An angel; d) The serpent

14. Blessed are they that mourn for they shall be

    _____.
    a) Comforted; b) Saved; c) Rich; d) Wise

15. What father almost sacrificed his own son on an altar?
    a) Abraham; b) David; c) Lot; d) Aaron

16. I have hidden your word in my

    _____ that I might not sin against you.
    a) Mind; b) Bible; *c) Heart*; d) Life

17. What did Jonah tell the sailors would happen if they threw him overboard?
    a) He would drown; b) He would walk on water; c) God would punish them; *d) The sea would be calm.*

18. Which book of the Bible has the most chapters?
    a) Genesis; *b) Psalms*; c) Proverbs; d) Revelation

19. What was the job of Paul?
    a) Tentmaker; b) Carpenter; c) Accountant; d) Tax collector

20. Who brought the Ark of the Covenant into Jerusalem?
    a) Moses; b) Solomon; *c) David*; d) Indiana Jones

Lost in the Translation

- The name Coca-Cola in China was first rendered as *Ke-kou-ke-la*. Unfortunately, the Coke company did not discover until after thousands of signs had been printed that the phrase means "bite the wax tadpole" or "female horse stuffed with wax" depending on the dialect. Coke then researched 40,000 Chinese characters and found a close phonetic equivalent, *Ko-kou-ko-le*, which can be loosely translated as "happiness in the mouth."

  Sometimes it's not just the words that get lost in the translation. Gerber is famous for selling baby food with a picture of a cute baby on the label. When they entered the African market, they decided to stick with the same packaging. Later they found out that since many people in Africa can't read, companies usually put pictures on the package of what's inside.

- An American T-shirt maker in Miami printed shirts for the Spanish market which promoted the Pope's visit. Instead of the desired "I Saw the Pope" in Spanish, the shirts proclaimed "I Saw the Potato."

- In Taiwan the translation of the Pepsi slogan "Come alive with the Pepsi Generation" came out as "Pepsi will bring your ancestors back from the dead."

- When translated into Chinese, the Kentucky Fried Chicken slogan "finger-lickin' good" came out as "eat your fingers off."

- A detour sign in Japan reads: Stop. Drive sideways.

- A sign in a Copenhagen airline ticket office says: We take your bags and send them in all directions.

- A sign at a Budapest zoo reads: Please do not feed the animals. If you have any suitable food, give it to the guard on duty.

Vital Verses

FOR GOD LOVED THE WORLD SO MUCH THAT HE GAVE HIS ONE AND ONLY SON THAT ANYONE WHO BELIEVES IN HIM SHALL NOT PERISH BUT HAVE ETERNAL LIFE (JOHN 3:16).

TO ALL WHO RECEIVED HIM, HE GAVE THE RIGHT TO BECOME CHILDREN OF GOD. (JOHN 1:12).

REPENT, THEN, AND TURN TO GOD, SO THAT YOUR SINS MAY BE WIPED OUT, THAT TIMES OF REFRESHING MAY COME FROM THE LORD (ACTS 3:19).

FOR ALL HAVE SINNED AND FALL SHORT OF THE GLORY OF GOD (ROMANS 3:23).

I AM THE WAY AND THE TRUTH AND THE LIFE. NO ONE COMES TO THE FATHER EXCEPT THROUGH ME (JOHN 14:6).

FOR THE WAGES OF SIN IS DEATH, BUT THE GIFT OF GOD IS ETERNAL LIFE IN CHRIST JESUS OUR LORD (ROMANS 6:23).

Devotions in Motion

WEEK FOUR: GO BY THE BOOK

DAY 1

FAST FACTS

Take yourself to Psalm 119:105.

God Says

It was a cold night in early September, and Jan sat shivering in the tent. Oh man, she thought, I really have to go to the bathroom!

Unfortunately, on this hastily planned camping trip no one had thought to bring a flashlight. Finally, though, Jan could stand it no longer.

"I can't wait for daylight," she said aloud as she got up quickly and stumbled out of the tent.

But as careful as she was during her daring trip to find the camp bathrooms, she stumbled and tripped, got mixed up in her direction and actually ended up back at the tent, where she finally gave up hope completely—and ended up using a poison oak bush for a restroom, which explains why she is not at school today.

And all because she didn't have a flashlight!

I Do

More important than a flashlight on a camping trip is God's Word. When has God's Word shown you the truth and comforted you?

How can you comfort others with what you have learned this week?

FOLD HERE ---

DAY 4

FAST FACTS

Spear Hebrews 4:12,13.

God Says

"Scalpel please," said Dr. Spurtenbludenguts to her assistant, Nurse John Doughboy. Now, Nurse John Doughboy was new to the surgical ward, so he gave the clamps to Dr. Spurtenbludenguts instead.

"No, no," Dr. Spurtenbludenguts corrected the mistaken Nurse John Doughboy.

"I need the scalpel. Let me describe it for you. It is a very sharp, knifelike tool that surgeons use to open a patient up. Without the scalpel, I cannot see what is inside this patient and correct the problem that is ailing him."

"Aaaah," said Nurse John Doughboy, handing her the scalpel.

"Now we'd better hurry up," said Dr. Spurtenbludenguts, because it looks like our patient is waking up!"

I Do

Like the scalpel in this story, God uses His Word to open us up and help us see what is wrong inside of us. While this is often painful, it is also very helpful so that we can live full and healthy lives as we seek to follow Him. Has God ever used His Word to correct you or get you back on track? When and how?

This week, ask a friend or an adult you know about a time God used His Word in his or her life to correct him or her and help him or her through a difficult time. Make sure you share your story too.

Pulse

FAST FACTS

DAY 2

Head into Deuteronomy 11:18-21.

God Says

You can tell a lot about a person by what they put on the walls in their room. We surround ourselves with the things that are important to us. What is on the walls of your bedroom or the walls of friends? Pictures of friends and family? Maybe posters of celebrities, sports heroes, music groups or solo artists? Perhaps you have even decorated your room with trophies and ribbons you've won from various events and activities.

I Do

God wants us to make His Word important to us too. Why? Because it guides us in decision making, reminds us of His love for us and teaches us about who He is.

Find a Bible verse that has stuck in your mind and heart from these past few lessons and make a poster out of it for your room. Use lots of color and be creative!!

FOLD HERE -

QUICK QUESTIONS

DAY 3

Read Ephesians 6:10-18.

God Says

In the past, a coat of armor was critical for soldiers in battle—both for the sake of protection (the defense) and for attacking the enemy (the offense). Think of football pads! In the passage you have just read, Paul described Christians as people wearing armor in a battle, with each piece of armor being a different part of the Christian life.

What is the Bible—God's Word—depicted as?

Why do you think Paul chose this piece of a soldier's uniform for the Bible?

If you were Paul writing this letter to the Ephesians, what piece of a soldier's uniform would you have chosen to represent God's Word? Why?

I Do

Pretend you are writing to a group of Christian football players. How would you rewrite Ephesians 6:10-18 in a way that would be meaningful to them, using their football gear instead of a soldier's armor.

Then spend some time today thanking God for His written Word!

Peer Pressure

The Big Idea

The Holy Spirit gives us strength to resist negative peer pressure.

Session Aims

In this session you will guide students to:

*   Know how the Holy Spirit can help them when they face peer pressure;
*   Feel confident knowing that the Spirit is always with them;
*   Act on what the Holy Spirit tells them to do this week.

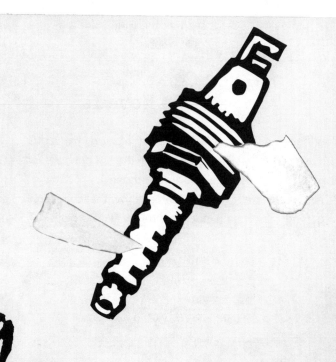

Plug in to Real Power

The Biggest Verse

"Then Peter, filled with the Holy Spirit, said to them: 'Rulers and elders of the people!'" Acts 4:8

Other Important Verses

1 Samuel 16:13; 2 Chronicles 16:9; Psalm 118:22; Isaiah 41:10; Matthew 10:17-20; Luke 11:13; John 10:14; 14:16,17; Acts 3:1-10; 4:5-20; 15:32; Romans 8:26; Galatians 5:22,23

STEP 1

MOVING IN

This step helps students see that the Holy Spirit is always there to help when they're in trouble.

Option 1  Move It

You'll need An adult volunteer, a pair of sturdy handcuffs and a crisp $10 bill (don't worry; there's only a *slim* chance that you'll actually lose your money).

Ahead of time, let the volunteer know that the secret to getting out of the handcuffs is to say "Please help."

> **What!?** You don't have a pair of handcuffs? Every self-respecting youth worker should have a pair. Most novelty shops carry them, but make sure you get sturdy ones that really work—you never know when you might need them!

Greet students and show them the handcuffs. Explain that there is a secret to getting out of these handcuffs—whoever can figure out the secret will win $10. Ask for volunteers (check the pulse of anyone not raising his or her hand!). Select a volunteer and place the handcuffs on him or her (tighten them securely, but comfortably). Give the signal and allow 30 seconds for the student to remove the handcuffs. Repeat the process for several students (no one should be able to figure out the secret—this is why you'll need a sturdy pair of handcuffs).

After several students have failed, invite the adult volunteer to come forward and demonstrate the secret; then explain: **The secret to getting out of this situation was simply asking for help from the person with the key. Life can be that way too; sometimes we face difficult situations where people are pressuring us to do something we know is wrong and we feel like we're all alone. The truth is that we're *not* alone. As we'll see today, God has promised that His Spirit will be with us to help during those hard times when we're pressured and tempted to do the wrong thing.**

Option 2  Chat Room

You'll need An adult volunteer, money for a bribe (see the details below to decide how much you'll want to have on hand), a hammer, a breakable item (one that appears valuable, but really isn't) and an old towel large enough to wrap the item in. **Note:** You can pick up inexpensive glassware—vase, goblet, picture frame, etc.—at discount or thrift stores, usually for less than a dollar.)

Ahead of time, inform the adult volunteer that his or her role will be to tell the student not to break the item.

Greet students and ask a female student (preferably a bit shy) to come forward. Hold up the item you brought and explain: _____ (name of someone that students know) **gave me this** _____ (item) **as a gift a while back. Right now I'm really mad at** (him/her) **for** _____ (reason you might be mad) **and I don't want this** _____ (item) **anymore. *I* can't break it, because if** _____ (name) **ever finds out it's broken, I have to be able to truthfully say that *I* didn't break it. So I have a solution: I'll have someone *else* do it!**

Offer the student a quarter to break the item for you. Chances are she'll refuse. Try to put the hammer in her hands and really put the pressure on her to help you out. If she still refuses (which she almost invariably will), raise the stakes by offering more money—go as high as you can afford.

As the bribe amount rises, get the group to help you put the pressure on by asking: **What do you think? Should she help me out here? Should she break it?** Lead the group in a chant: **Break it! Break it! Break it!** At this point, the adult volunteer should gently counteract the pressure of the group on the girl—perhaps even standing between you and her to protect her from the pressure. Other students (typically boys) will run up and offer to break it for you, but *don't let them*. Keep the pressure building until the girl either breaks the item or until you reach the limit of the amount you can offer. If she gave into the pressure, ask: **Why did you give up and break it?** If she held fast to her decision not to break it, ask: **What kept you from breaking it?**

Discuss with the group:

Would you have broken it? Why or why not?

How much money would it have taken for you to break the item?

What did you think of how _____ (name of adult volunteer) **stood by** _____ (name of girl) **and told her not to break it?**

Have you ever had someone come to your defense when you were being pressured to do something wrong?

Explain: **Having that quiet voice in the midst of complete pressure is what the Holy Spirit does for us in our lives. Today we're going to learn about how God's Holy Spirit is there to help us when we face difficult situations and how He helps us know how to respond to the pressure.**

Option 3 — Fun and Games

You'll need A towel.

Greet students and have everyone sit in one circle. Explain that you're going to play a game of Towel Toss.[1] Select a student to be It and ask him or her to sit in the middle of the circle. Give the towel to one of the students in the circle and explain that when you give the signal, students forming the circle should toss the towel back and forth to keep It from touching either the towel or the person holding it. If the person in the middle catches the towel or touches someone holding it, the person who threw it or was touched is now It.

Play for a few minutes; then bring another student into the middle of the circle. The new student and It will now work as a team. Begin again and allow several minutes for students to play; then end the game and explain: **Sometimes life can be similar to this game; we can feel like we're in the middle and that everyone else is doing something against what we're trying to do. Just as someone came in to help the person in the middle during the game, God's Holy Spirit helps us by being there when we face difficult situations. Today we're going to look at how the Holy Spirit even helps us know what to** *say* **when we face pressure situations.**

STEP 2 — MOVING UP

This step helps students see that the Holy Spirit will help them to know what to say when they face negative peer pressure.

Option 1 — Move It

You'll need Several Bibles, lots of room for students to lie down flat, a balloon for each student (bigger balloons are better), a CD or audiocassette of fast music and a CD or audiocassette player.

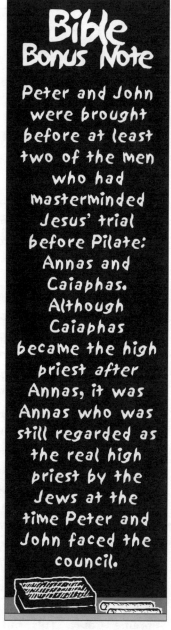

Bible Bonus Note

Peter and John were brought before at least two of the men who had masterminded Jesus' trial before Pilate: Annas and Caiaphas. Although Caiaphas became the high priest after Annas, it was Annas who was still regarded as the real high priest by the Jews at the time Peter and John faced the council.

Ahead of time, a few days before the meeting, blow up and tie one balloon so that it will be at least partly deflated for this exercise.

Distribute balloons and instruct students to blow them up and tie them off. Have everyone lie down on their backs on the floor and explain that they are going to try to keep all the balloons up in the air for as long as they can *without lifting their backs off the floor.* Hands, feet or any other body part can be used and students can even shuffle around the floor on their backs, but they must keep their backs on the floor's surface. Give the signal to begin by starting the music and see how long students can keep all of the balloons in the air.

Let students play a few rounds to get a best time; then have students sit on their balloons and pop them all at once. Show the balloon you prepared a few days before and explain: **When we face peer pressure, it's kind of like this balloon. It is deflated because the air pressure on the outside of the balloon is greater than the air pressure inside.** Blow up a new balloon and continue: **A new balloon stays inflated because the pressure on the inside equals the pressure on the outside. When we face negative peer pressure, we need to rely on the Holy Spirit to give us the internal pressure needed to help us stand firm against what's being pushed on us from the outside.**

Distribute Bibles and share the story found in Acts 4:5-20 of Peter and John appearing before the Sanhedrin to answer for healing the beggar by the temple (see Acts 3:1-10). Explain: **The Sanhedrin was comprised of rulers, elders and teachers of the law; a kind of Israel Supreme Court. This put Peter and John—two unschooled and ordinary men** (see Acts 4:13)—**up against some pretty smart people. Because they were filled with the Holy Spirit, however, what should have been a pretty intimidating situation was actually easy for them to handle. The Holy Spirit gave them the right words to say when they had to respond. Not only were they able to share the story of Jesus' crucifixion and resurrection, but they were also able to show how Jesus fulfilled Old Testament prophecy, an important element in early Christian sermons and defenses** (see Acts 4:8-11). **They were so compelled by the Holy Spirit to speak that even when the Sanhedrin commanded them not to share any more about Jesus, they said they could not "help speaking about what we have seen and heard"** (Acts 4:20).

Continue: **God can and will give us the right words to say. All we have to do is to listen for Him. Next we're going to discover how we can hear the voice of God through the Holy Spirit.**

Option 2 — Chat Room

You'll need Several Bibles, a TV, a VCR and the video *Liar, Liar.*

Ahead of time, cue the video approximately 22 minutes from the opening graphic to the scene where the main character (played by Jim Carrey) enters the courtroom. The clip you'll be playing will last approximately four minutes.

> CAUTION
> This video contains sexual references. Carefully preview the clip you'll be using for this exercise and edit (fast forward) as appropriate for your group.

Play the video clip; then discuss:

Have you ever had a time when you couldn't say what you wanted to say?

Have you ever had to speak in front of a group of people? What happened?

Explain: **Researchers say that the number one fear of people in America is public speaking (number two is death). So people are more afraid of speaking at funerals than being the dead person at them. Weird, huh?** Discuss: **Are you afraid of speaking in front of groups? Why?**

Explain: **We have all had times when we can't really express what we want to say. Maybe it's when you were on the phone with that special guy or girl, or maybe it was when people were trying to pressure you into doing something you know you shouldn't. There's a great story in the Bible about two guys who faced some pressure, and knew exactly what to say—because God's Spirit filled them.**

Distribute Bibles and ask four volunteers to read through Acts 4:5-20 (each reading four verses). Add the background information found in Step 2, Option 1 regarding the charges against Peter and John and the Sanhedrin's role in society. Discuss:

What enabled Peter to speak so boldly in Acts 4:8? The Holy Spirit.

How would you summarize what Peter said in verses 8 through 11? He explained the story of Jesus' crucifixion and resurrection—and how Jesus fulfilled Old Testament prophecy from Psalm 118:22.

How would you describe Peter and John? Ordinary men filled with the extraordinary Holy Spirit (see Acts 4:13).

How did Peter and John respond to the Sanhedrin's command to stop speaking about Jesus? They refused to stop, claiming that they could not "help speaking about what we have seen and heard" (Acts 4:20).

Transition to the next step: **Isn't it cool that the Holy Spirit can actually give us words to say when we're in difficult situations? Now we're going to find out how we can listen to what the Holy Spirit says to us.**

Option 3 Pulse Points

You'll need Several Bibles, a TV, a VCR, the video *Raiders of the Lost Ark,* a wind instrument (trumpet, flute, etc.) and someone who can play it well.

Ahead of time, cue the video approximately 58 minutes from the opening graphic to the two-minute scene where Indiana Jones (played by Harrison Ford) and his friend find the hidden room and are confronted with Indiana's least favorite creatures—snakes.

The Big Idea

The Holy Spirit is able to help us in times of peer pressure.

The Big Question

What does the Holy Spirit do to help us stand against peer pressure?

Briefly share the story of how Peter and John healed the crippled beggar in Acts 3:1-10, emphasizing God's amazing ability to work through others—in this case, Peter and John—to change people's lives.

Distribute Bibles and ask five volunteers to help read through Acts 4:5-20 in the following manner: Three of them will read as the rulers, elders and teachers of the law; the other two will read as Peter and John. You will serve as the narrator, reading everything that isn't in quotation marks. When the passage indicates that a group of people spoke, the students will read as a group.

After the reading, explain: **Isn't it interesting that Peter and John were put in jail for doing something good? The religious leaders didn't like their healing a man who had been crippled for over 40 years. Even today, sometimes people don't like it when we do good. It can be hard to face people when they criticize us for doing good or try to pressure us into doing something wrong. Peter and John had a secret that made the pressure they faced seem pretty powerless—the Holy Spirit. The Holy Spirit gave Peter and John at least two weapons against that pressure.**

1. The Holy Spirit gave them courage.

Peter and John were facing more pressure than people today typically face; they had just seen the same men that they faced engineer Jesus' death on the cross.

Youth Leader Tip

When leading a group of more than 10 students, consider dividing students into small groups for discussions. This can help prevent more dominant students from taking over and help students who might not respond in a large group to feel more comfortable in a smaller setting.

In fact, just a few chapters later, the apostles were all whipped for speaking about Jesus. Later, most of them were killed for their faith. The courage Peter and John had to stand up to this intense pressure came directly from the presence of the Holy Spirit.

Explain: **Courage isn't the absence of fear—it's the ability to face our fears.** Play the video clip; then continue: **Indy's friend suggested that Indy go into the room first. This gave him two choices: show courage and go ahead or wimp out and refuse. He chose to face his tremendous fear of snakes and go in. Lots of circumstances can evoke fear. At those times when we're afraid, we can ask the Holy Spirit to give us the courage we need—and count on Him to provide it.**

2. The Holy Spirit gave them words.

Explain: **Sometimes it's hard to know what to say when people are pressuring us. We can feel like idiots when we try to resist negative peer pressure.** Jesus warned Peter and John that they would face a situation like this. In Matthew 10:17-20, He said, "Be on your guard against men; they will hand you over to the local councils and flog you in their synagogues. On my account you will be brought before governors and kings as witnesses to them and to the Gentiles. But when they arrest you, do not worry about what to say or how to say it. At that time you will be given what to say, for it will not be you speaking, but the Spirit of your Father speaking through you."

Explain that God wants to do the same with us. If we are constantly growing in our relationship with Him and remain open to the Holy Spirit working in and through us, He will give us the words to say when we face pressure situations—just like He did for Peter and John.

Hold up the musical instrument and explain: **This instrument can't play by itself; it needs someone to blow air into it.** Invite the person who can play the instrument to do so; then continue: **When the Holy Spirit speaks through us, it's like we're the instrument and God is playing His music through us. We can actually speak the words of God to people who are trying to pressure us. Right now we're going to look at how we can actually listen for the voice of the Holy Spirit in our lives.**

STEP 3

This step will help students learn to listen to the Holy Spirit.

Option 1 Chat Room

You'll need Some loud students (a tall order, we know!).

Have students form a large circle; then assign each student a partner directly across from him or her in the circle. Instruct students to sit down where they are and proceed to find out three pieces of personal trivia from their across-the-room partners: 1) middle name; 2) favorite dessert; and 3) favorite musical group. Explain that partners can communicate however they want, but they are *not* allowed to move from where they're sitting. Give the signal to begin and allow one minute of information gathering; then give the signal to stop and discuss:

How many of you found out all three things about your partner?

What techniques did you use to communicate? Lip reading, sign language, shouting louder than everyone else.

What made the communication difficult? Too much noise in the room, too many conflicting messages.

How does this activity relate to our topic of hearing the Holy Spirit? The Holy Spirit usually communicates as the still, small voice; we often don't allow ourselves to be quiet enough to hear Him.

What can we do to better hear the Holy Spirit? Spend quiet time alone; don't immediately turn on the radio or TV when you walk in a room; pray and ask God to speak to you; then wait and listen.

Continue: **We're going to end this session by looking at how we can be ready to act when the Holy Spirit speaks to us.**

NOTES

Option 2  Real Life

You'll need Just this *libro* (that's "book" in Spanish).

Share the following case study:

Ethan has gone to church for as long as he can remember, but he doesn't pray or read his Bible very much. In fact, the only time he *really* prays is when he's in trouble and needs God to bail him out.

Ethan wanted to earn some extra money, so he took a paper route near his home. Most people paid when he went to their house collecting, but Mrs. Sanchez worked evenings, so she always left her money in the mailbox for Ethan to pick up. Even though the paper cost $15 a month, Mrs. Sanchez always left him a $20 bill—she had told Ethan that she would give him an extra $5 every month if he brought the paper right up to the front door instead of leaving it on the curb.

One day, Ethan picked up the envelope in the mailbox as usual, and when he opened it, he noticed there were actually *two* $20 bills stuck together in the envelope.

Ethan wasn't sure what to do—had Mrs. Sanchez made a mistake by putting the extra $20 in the envelope?

Ethan asked his friend, Luke, who replied, "Who cares if she meant to put it in there? It's yours now! It's not like she's hurting for money!"

Lauren, Ethan's sister, told him that he should definitely give it back, but he thought maybe she was just jealous because he had the extra money and she didn't.

His mom said, "Why don't you just talk to her and ask her if it was a gift?" But he thought it would be pretty embarrassing to ask her about it.

Ethan was so confused!

Discuss:

What do you think God might have told Ethan if he had asked? He should go talk to Mrs. Sanchez so he would know for sure.

Ethan was hearing lots of advice from many sources. How could he have practiced listening for *God's* voice? He could have spent more time walking and talking with God instead of turning to Him only when he was in trouble.

Explain: **It's important to be close to God so that we can hear the voice of His Spirit when He speaks. Let's take a look at how to be ready to act when He speaks to us.**

Option 3  Tough Questions

1. **How does the Holy Spirit speak to us?** The Holy Spirit speaks in many ways. Most people don't hear an audible voice, but some do. Often we get an impression from the Holy Spirit about what to do—it just seems to be the right thing to do. Sometimes He speaks to us through Scripture or through a friend, relative or pastor.

2. **What's the difference between the gifts of the Spirit and the fruit of the Spirit?** The gifts are generally supernatural manifestations of the work of God (i.e., teaching, prophecy, healing, etc.), while the fruit of the Spirit is the changes in our attitudes and actions to be more like Christ (see Galatians 5:22,23).

3. **What if I don't feel the Holy Spirit in me—does this mean He isn't there?** God has promised that the Holy Spirit will be with us always—even when we don't feel His presence. Sometimes, though, we don't feel His presence because of unconfessed sin or not spending time with God or being too busy to listen.

4. **Will the Holy Spirit ever lead someone to do something that is against what the Bible teaches?** No, no, no, no, no! On the contrary, the *best* way to determine if the Holy Spirit is speaking to us is to find out if what we are hearing is in line with what the Bible teaches.

Explain: **Unless you're like Moses and you encounter a burning bush on your way to school one day, the only way to hear the Holy Spirit speaking to you is to dedicate yourself to following Christ. Let's take a closer look at listening for God's voice.**

STEP 4
MOVING OUT

This step will help students live out what the Holy Spirit prompts them to do.

Option 1 Light the Fire

You'll need Gift Bibles (optional), an adult volunteer (to make the game more difficult, the volunteer should be the same gender as you) and space for junior highers to run around.

Explain that you're going to end this session with a game called "Seasick". Here's how to play: Students must run to a wall in the room corresponding to a nautical term. Huh? OK, "bow" is the front; "stern" is the back; "port" is the left side and "starboard" is the right! If, at any time, you call out "Cap'n on deck," students must stand still where they are and salute. The last person to salute is out. Not so hard, right? Wrong. The adult volunteer is *also* going to be calling out commands. Anyone caught obeying his or her commands is out.

Play until you have a winner; then explain: **This game demonstrates what Jesus meant when He said, "I know my sheep and my sheep know me"** (John 10:14). **You've listened to my voice during this whole session; you're familiar with it. If you listened very carefully during the game, you would recognize my voice over any others. It's the same with God; the closer we get to Jesus, the more we hear the voice of His Spirit.**

Use the following option to close the session or simply close in prayer, asking the Holy Spirit to speak to each of the students and to make them ready to obey when He speaks.

CLOSING OPTION: Use this opportunity to invite students who've not yet accepted Jesus into their lives as Lord and Savior to do so now. Explain: **There may be some of you right now who are feeling the Holy Spirit calling you to submit your lives to God. You've tried to live on our own and it hasn't worked out so well. You need a Savior to help you to overcome your sin and have a right relationship with God.**

Ask everyone to close their eyes, bow their heads in prayer and invite those who want to ask Jesus into their lives to raise their hands and silently repeat the following prayer: **Dear Lord Jesus, I know that I'm a sinner. I know that I can't possibly have eternal life in heaven without accepting You as my Lord and Savior. Please come into my heart, Jesus, and wash me clean from my sins. Make me new in You and help me to begin a new life right now following Your guidance. Amen.**

Invite those who committed their lives to Christ just now to see you after the session. Give them a gift Bible. Be sure to note their names and phone numbers or e-mail addresses so that you can connect with them in the upcoming weeks to encourage their walk in Christ!

Option 2 Fired Up

You'll need Two pieces of Juicy Fruit gum for each student, copies of "Juicy Fruit—Galatians 5:22,23" (p. 76) and pens or pencils.

Distribute "Juicy Fruit—Galatians 5:22,23" and pens or pencils. Explain: **When we're faced with peer pressure situations, the qualities of the Holy Spirit should show through us. How do we know what they are?** Explain that one of the best checklists to see if the Holy Spirit is working through us is found in Galatians 5:22,23.

Allow three minutes for students to complete the handout; then divide the group into small groups of four to six. Members in each group are to share the area that they feel they're doing the best in and the area they most need to work on.

Instruct groups to close in prayer, each member praying for the person on his or her right. After the prayer, distribute two pieces of gum to each student. They can chew one piece now, but challenge them to carry the other piece with them throughout the week to remind them to show the fruit of the Spirit in their lives.

Option 3  Spread the Fire

You'll need Five copies of "Living the Life" (p. 77).

Ahead of time, arrange for four students and one adult to play the roles in the skit and provide copies for them to practice their parts a couple of days in advance. They don't necessarily have to memorize their lines, but it would be nice if they could read them without stumbling over the words.

Introduce the drama and act as the narrator. Have the four students act out Part One; then explain to the audience that they're going to watch a replay of the same situation, but this time they're going to see what happens when Jared carries on a conversation with the Holy Spirit as he goes through it.

After Part Two, conclude: **Even peer pressure situations can turn into good evangelistic opportunities—if we are open to the Holy Spirit working through us. The key is to carry on a conversation with God—through prayer—while facing the pressure.**

Close in prayer, asking God to help students be more connected to the Holy Spirit in tough situations this week, so that others will notice that they are different!

Note
1. Adapted from Jim Burns, gen. ed., Mark Simone and Joel Lusz, comp., "Towel Toss," *Fresh Ideas: Games, Crowdbreakers and Community Builders* (Ventura, CA: Gospel Light, 1997), p. 154.

NOTES

Juicy Fruit--Galatians 5:22,23

How much fruit of the Spirit do you show in your life? Rate each fruit on a scale of 1 (*Help! I need a map to the spiritual produce aisle!*) to 10 (*Gonna have to open up a fruit stand pretty soon!*).

Love

_____ I willingly sacrifice my own desires in order to serve others.

Joy

_____ I have joy deep inside regardless of the situation on the outside.

Peace

_____ I feel an inner quiet no matter what situation I find myself in.

Patience

_____ I don't get angry when people try to upset me and I don't entertain thoughts of getting even.

Kindness

_____ I help people in need.

Goodness

_____ I do the morally right things and obey God's commands.

Faithfulness

_____ I am trustworthy and reliable.

Gentleness

_____ I'm not harsh or impatient with people.

Self-Control

_____ I exercise discipline and resist temptation.

Living the Life

Cast

Jared, a seventh-grade Christian
Keith, his non-Christian best friend
Ryan and Karl, their classmates
The Holy Spirit

It's Saturday and Karl, Jared and Keith are all at Ryan's house playing video games and hanging out.

Karl: Man, this game rocks! Check it out--I just blew that guy's head off!

Ryan: Hey, you guys want something to drink? Soda, water . . . beer?

Karl: *(Yells over his shoulder.)* Dude! I'm into that. Grab me a cold one.

Ryan: What about you guys?

Keith: OK, I guess. It can't hurt to have just one.

Ryan: Jared? Hello? *Jared!*

Jared: Nah, I don't think so.

Karl: *(Suddenly interested.)* Why not? Are you a baby? Does the baby need some milk instead?

Jared: I'm *not* a baby! I just don't want any beer.

Ryan: Oh, that's right. Jared's a *church boy*.

Jared: Knock it off!

Karl: I get it. Jared's a church *baby*!

Karl and Ryan: Church baby! Church baby! Church baby!

Jared runs out of the house, embarrassed.

Second Version

It's Saturday and Karl, Jared and Keith are all at Ryan's house playing video games and hanging out. The Holy Spirit is there too, talking with Jared and guiding him.

Karl: Man, this game rocks! Check it out--I just blew that guy's head off!

Ryan: Hey, you guys want something to drink? Soda, water . . . beer?

Karl: *(Yells over his shoulder.)* Dude! I'm into that. Grab me a cold one.

Everyone else freezes while Jared talks with the Holy Spirit.

Jared: Oh, great. What am I supposed to do now?

Holy Spirit: It's OK, Jared. Let's use this situation to enlighten your friends a little. Are you ready? I'll give you the courage and even the words to plant some seeds in your friends' hearts, OK?

Jared: OK!

Everyone reanimates.

Ryan: What about you guys?

Keith: OK, I guess. It can't hurt to have just one.

Ryan: Jared? Hello? *Jared!*

Holy Spirit: Just give him a simple "No, thanks."

Jared: *(To Ryan.)* No, thanks.

Karl: *(Suddenly interested.)* Why not? Are you a baby? Does the baby need some milk instead?

Holy Spirit: You know, sometimes people pick on other people because they're insecure about themselves. Karl's afraid the others won't like him if he says no. So don't play into it.

Jared: *(Thinks about it.)* Wow, I never thought of it that way. *(To Karl.)* Actually, I do like milk--but you don't have to be a baby to not drink beer. We're too young to be doing it, that's all.

Ryan: Oh, that's right. Jared's a *church boy*. This is a *church* thing.

Holy Spirit: Jared, it's not a church thing; it's a God thing. Tell them about Me.

Jared: No, it's a God thing. It's about my relationship with Him and obeying Him.

Karl: *(Rolls his eyes.)* Oh, puhleeze!

Holy Spirit: Don't let him get to you. Share about Ephesians 5:18 that you read this morning.

Jared: I can't change what you think. But the Bible says, "Don't get drunk.... Instead, be filled with the Spirit." Being filled with God's Spirit gives me happiness and peace--*and* I won't wake up with a hangover in the morning!

Karl: *Whatever*, church baby. You don't have to preach at me.

Holy Spirit: Jared, you've been a good witness, but now it's time to go.

Jared: I guess I should go. Thanks for inviting me, Ryan, but I don't think I should hang around if you guys are going to drink.

Keith: *(Jumps up.)* Hold up! I'll come with you. *(As they are walking home.)* Wow, no one's ever said anything like that to Karl before.

Jared: Well, I had some help. *(Looks at Holy Spirit.)*

Keith: Yeah, OK. Hey, did you really mean all that stuff about being filled with the Spirit?

Jared: Sure did. You want to hear some more?

Keith: *(Pauses and thinks about it; then smiles.)* Yeah, I do.

Jared: *(To Holy Spirit.)* OK, Holy Spirit, here we go!

Holy Spirit: Right by your side, Jared! I got your back!

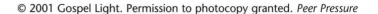

Devotions in Motion

WEEK FIVE: PLUG IN TO REAL POWER

DAY 1

QUICK QUESTIONS

Check out John 14:16,17.

God Says

Have you ever gone to camp and had a camp counselor? Maybe you have counselors at your school. Did you know that God has given you His Spirit as a counselor? What is the job of a counselor anyway?

- ☐ To tell you whatever you want to hear whenever you want to hear it
- ☐ To tell you the truth, to help you and to comfort you
- ☐ To be your personal butler and make your every heart's desire come true

I Do

Spend some time thanking God for the gift of His Holy Spirit. Talk to God about some of the situations you are in where you feel peer pressure—and ask Him for this help!

- - - - - - FOLD HERE -

DAY 4

QUICK QUESTIONS

Flip over to Galatians 5:16,17.

God Says

Every day we make a ton of choices. Write down five choices that you have made so far today, such as what clothes to wear, what to have for breakfast and so on

The passage you have just read says that you have yet another choice to make that you may not have even known about. What is it?

I Do

It is easy to know which is the better choice in Galatians 5:16,17, but it is not always easy to make the right choice! To encourage you, though, when you choose to live by the Spirit, know that it becomes easier to make that choice every day. Take a few minutes to memorize Galatians 5:16,17.

FAST FACTS
Trot over to 1 Corinthians 2:1-13.

God Says
Jessie hangs out at school with a group of friends who like to pull pranks. It has been fun in the past—like the time they hung Sarah's teddy bear collection by their necks in her closet or when they TP'd the youth pastor's house (helping to clean it up the next morning, of course). But this time Jessie doesn't feel so good about their prank. Jessie has a bad feeling in his stomach as they all prepared to go out to the teachers' parking lot and key Mrs. Santiago's car. Heart beating, mind racing, Jessie swallows hard and . . .

I Do
What would you do or say at this point? Sometimes a bad situation can become an opportunity for us to reveal God's truth to our friends. The great thing is that God doesn't put us out there on our own but gives us guidance by his Holy Spirit. That's why Jessie wasn't feeling so good about this prank. If you were in Jessie's position, what would you say to your friends?

FOLD HERE

FAST FACTS
Cruise to Zechariah 4:6.

God Says
Have you ever tried to break a bad habit? Well, Jamie had a problem with cursing. She cursed all the time—she had a total potty mouth! One day, she asked a friend to pull her hair (to really yank a handful!) every time she said a curse word. And she stopped cursing—when her friend was around to pull her hair, that is. The truth is that when we try to do things in our own strength—like breaking bad habits or standing up to peer pressure—we will fail. If we don't fail right away, we certainly will down the line. We need God's Spirit to work in us and make us strong!

I Do
Train yourself to rely on the Holy Spirit today! Think of two situations in which it is hard for you not to follow the crowd. Write down those two situations and today's verse on a small piece of paper and carry it with you to remind you to pray for strength and guidance in those times. When you get into those situations, pray at that moment too!

Peer Pressure

The Big Idea

Knowing who you are in Christ and what you believe helps you resist peer pressure.

Session Aims

In this session you will guide students to:

- Examine their beliefs about their own identity in Christ;
- Sense confidence in who they are as followers of Jesus;
- Feel convicted to act differently this week because of their beliefs.

The Biggest Verse

"About midnight Paul and Silas were praying and singing hymns to God, and the other prisoners were listening to them." Acts 16:25

Other Important Verses

Mark 9:24; John 20:27; Acts 9:3-6; 16:16-36; Romans 12:1,2; 2 Timothy 1:12; James 2:23

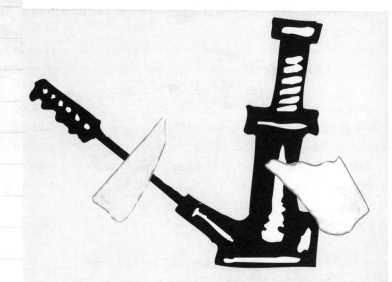

You've Got to Stand for Something or You'll Fall for Anything

STEP
MOVING IN

This step will help students look at who they are and what they believe.

Option 1 — Move It

You'll need Self-adhesive name tags, a felt-tip pen, a CD or cassette of lively music and a CD or cassette player.

Ahead of time, prepare a name tag for each student, using the names of famous people that students will know (i.e., actors, singers, authors, sports stars, etc.—don't forget *yourself*!).

Greet students as they come in and stick a name tag on the back of each student. Explain that each student has to figure out whose name is on the tag on his or her back by asking only yes or no questions. (For example, "Am I an actor?") No misleading answers allowed!

Once a student has correctly identified the name on his or her tag, he or she should act like that famous person. Encourage students to ham it up! Start the music and enjoy the confusion!

Allow time for all students to figure out whose famous name is on their backs and to act like that person; then settle everyone down and explain: **Who we think we are definitely changes how we act. In our everyday lives, sometimes it's hard to really know who we are. We might know our names, what our favorite color is, how tall we are and where we live—but we don't always know what we really believe. Today, we're going to see how knowing who you are and what you really believe makes all the difference in how you respond to peer pressure—and how your identity determines your actions.**

NOTES

Option 2 — Chat Room

You'll need A large sheet of poster board, several copies of magazines featuring celebrities (you can probably get some older ones from your doctor's or dentist's office), scissors, glue, paper, pens or pencils and candy prizes.

Ahead of time, find pictures of at least 10 famous people and carefully cut out just the eye area of each picture. (**Important:** Note the name of the person the eyes belong to on the back as you go!)

Also ahead of time, number each picture (yes, name *and* number). Got it? OK. Create an identity key for yourself by noting each picture's number and the corresponding person's identity on a piece of paper. But wait, we're not done yet! Now you need to glue the pictures on the poster board and write *only* each picture's number below as you go. (*Now* do you see why you need the identity key?)

Greet students and ask: **How much can you tell about people just by looking at their eyes?** Distribute paper and pens or pencils and point out the poster board. Explain that when you give the signal, students are going to try to guess the famous owner of each pair of eyes. Give the signal to begin and allow a couple of minutes for students to guess as many of the famous names as they can.

> **Note:** You can make this exercise a little easier by providing a list of the famous people for students to choose from.

Allow a couple of minutes; then give the signal for students to stop writing. Call out the correct identity of each pair of eyes and award candy to the student(s) who identified the most. Discuss:

What does "the eyes are the windows of the soul" mean? It means that you can sometimes tell a lot about a person's character (honesty, integrity) from his or her eyes.

How do you feel when someone looks directly into your eyes for a long time? Sometimes it can feel as though the person is looking straight through us to our innermost thoughts and feelings.

Explain: **Although our eyes can tell a lot about us, our beliefs tell even more. Our beliefs affect our** actions—and our actions reveal the most about our character. Today we're going to look at how knowing who you really are determines how you act when faced with peer pressure.

Option 3  Fun and Games

You'll need A big, thick blanket (one that can't be seen through) and two adult helpers.

Greet students and explain that they're going to play a recognition game. Divide students into two teams; then, one at a time, have every team member state his or her name so that everyone on both teams can hear. After everyone has been introduced, ask the two adult helpers to hold the blanket like a curtain between the teams with the bottom just barely touching the ground. One at a time, each team will send a member forward to stand and face the blanket. On the count of three, the adults will drop the blanket and the first player to correctly say the name of the other player wins that round. The opposing teammate must now go over to the side of the winner. Play until one team wins everyone to its side; then regroup and explain:

Our names are important to us. We like it when people remember our names, because they are a reflection of who we are. But we are a lot more than just our names. Today we're going to look at how knowing who you really are determines how you act when faced with peer pressure.

STEP 2 MOVING UP

This step will help students see that their identity—who they are—determines their actions.

Option 1  Move It

You'll need A Bible, a table, a glass of water, building blocks and 10 action figures (the more outrageous, the better *and* they should have removable pieces of clothing) to represent the following characters: Paul, Silas, a slave girl, the slave girl's owner, a magistrate, two guards, the jailer and the jailer's wife and son.

Ask for several volunteers to help you act out a Bible story about Paul and Silas using the action figures (just for fun, assign two figures per volunteer) and one or two volunteers to build a jail while the action is going on. Read Acts 16:16-36 and have the volunteers use the action figures where indicated. When you reach the part where there's an earthquake, reach over and shake the table violently so that the jail falls apart. Use the glass of water for baptizing the jailer's family.

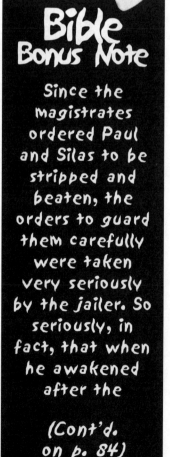

Youth Leader Tip

Nothing impresses a junior high student who is new to your ministry more than you remembering his or her name. There aren't usually many other adults in their lives who make an effort to learn their names, so when we do it, it shows them that we really care about them as people.

Bible Bonus Note

Since the magistrates ordered Paul and Silas to be stripped and beaten, the orders to guard them carefully were taken very seriously by the jailer. So seriously, in fact, that when he awakened after the

(Cont'd. on p. 84)

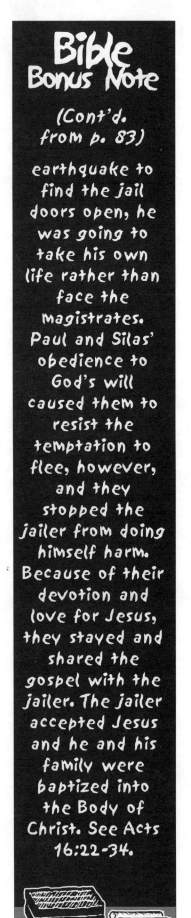

Bible Bonus Note

(Cont'd. from p. 83)

earthquake to find the jail doors open, he was going to take his own life rather than face the magistrates. Paul and Silas' obedience to God's will caused them to resist the temptation to flee, however, and they stopped the jailer from doing himself harm. Because of their devotion and love for Jesus, they stayed and shared the gospel with the jailer. The jailer accepted Jesus and he and his family were baptized into the Body of Christ. See Acts 16:22-34.

When you're done with the story, emphasize how amazing it was that even after Paul and Silas had been beaten, whipped and thrown in jail, they were able to pray and sing hymns. They didn't wallow in self-pity over what had happened to them. They believed that God loved them and would take care of them no matter what. Explain: **Even after the miraculous earthquake, Paul and Silas knew it would be wrong to leave the prison because the jailer would be killed for letting them escape. So they stayed, shared their faith with him, and he and his family became part of God's family.**

Paul and Silas knew who they were—followers of Jesus. And their behavior in the jail really demonstrated their belief. Even in the midst of suffering and persecution, they continued to praise God and do what was right. They wouldn't give in to any pressure to relinquish their faith because they were confident in who they were and what they believed.

Challenge students to begin considering their own faith by asking: **Would your convictions stand up to the kind of pressures that Paul and Silas faced?** Continue: **Today we're going to look at how knowing who you really are determines how you act when faced with peer pressure.**

Option 2  Chat Room

You'll need Several Bibles.

Read the following Aesop's fable, titled "The Scorpion and the Frog":

> A scorpion and a frog meet on the bank of a stream and the scorpion asks the frog to carry him across on its back. The frog asks, "How do I know you won't sting me?" The scorpion replies, "Because if I sting you, I will die too."
>
> The frog, satisfied with the scorpion's answer, agrees to give the scorpion a ride.
>
> When they hit midstream, the scorpion stings the frog. The frog feels the onset of paralysis and starts to sink, knowing they both will drown, but has just enough time to gasp, "Why?"
>
> The scorpion replies, "It's my nature."

Discuss:

What did the scorpion mean when he said, "It's my nature?" He had to act according to what he was, even if it meant he would die.

Was the frog stupid to give the scorpion a ride across the river? Why or why not?

Do you think the scorpion knew he would end up stinging the frog? He may have wanted to believe he could refrain from acting on his natural instincts, so he chose to think he had everything under control.

Do people always act like who they are? People don't always act according to what they *say* they are or what they say they believe, but they almost always act in accordance with what they truly are and what they truly believe. The scorpion professed to be someone who would not sting the frog, but in the end he acted in character with who he truly was.

Distribute Bibles and ask students to turn to the story of Paul and Silas in Acts 16:16-36. Read through the passage as a group, each student reading one verse. Use the background information given in Step 2, Option 1 to explain that Paul and Silas acted according to their nature. They were followers of Jesus Christ, and no amount of pressure—not even physical pain—could make them act otherwise. In the midst of all that, they continued to pray, sing hymns and trust God.

Explain: **When the pressure is on, who we are determines how we act. We will act according to our true nature when people try to pressure us into doing things that we shouldn't. Will you be like Paul and Silas? They knew who they were in Christ and wouldn't give in to the pressure. Not only do we act according to our nature, but next we're going to look at how the strength of what we believe determines how strongly we can resist negative peer pressure.**

Option 3  Pulse Points

You'll need Several shirts that symbolize different aspects of your life (i.e., a casual shirt you like to hang out in, a dress shirt for church, a sports shirt, etc.), a small container of play dough and something that you can squeeze the play dough into.

Ahead of time, put on all of the shirts at once; hopefully students will only see one shirt at a time when you take it off. This should be obvious to you, but make sure you are wearing a T-shirt that you won't take off under all of your layers (or you're sure to get some phone calls from parents tomorrow!).

The Big Idea
Our identity and our beliefs can help us in tempting situations.

The Big Question
What do we need to know in order to be able to stand against tempting situations?

Share the story of Paul and Silas from Acts 16:16-36; then explain that there are two things we must know:

1. Know who you are.
Before his conversion, the apostle Paul was the biggest threat the new Christian church faced. In fact, Saul of Tarsus, as he was known then, was on his way to Damascus to take prisoners of all who followed Christ when he first met Jesus face-to-face (see Acts 9:3-6). After accepting Christ into his life, he became a new man; a man called "Paul" by Jesus Himself. Later on, when he was jailed, he knew that he was saved by Christ and could have a positive and worshipful attitude no matter what (see Acts 16:25).

Explain: **We're not usually as sure about who we are as Paul was after he accepted Jesus as his Lord and Savior. In fact, sometimes we act like totally different people depending on who we're around.** Use the shirts to illustrate as you continue: **We can act one way around our friends, another around our parents and another way at church. Pretty soon, it can become hard to figure out who we really are deep down—where it counts. Paul knew who he was—a follower of Jesus Christ and a missionary to the Gentiles—and he acted like it around everyone.**

2. Know what you believe.
Just as he knew who he was, Paul also knew what he believed. He believed that Jesus had died on the cross for the sins of mankind and that He had risen again. He knew that it was his belief that made the difference in his life and that this belief—this truth—would make the difference in the lives of others, including the jailer (see Acts 16:31).

Explain: **Paul provided a secret in the letter he wrote to the people in Rome. He said, "Do not conform any longer to the pattern of this world, but be transformed by the renewing of your mind" (Romans 12:2). In other words, don't let the world tell you what to believe and how to act.** Illustrate by squeezing the play dough into the container and continue: **If you don't want to get squeezed into the mold somebody else is trying to pressure you into, you need to be strong in your beliefs. Now let's take a look at how our responses to negative peer pressure depends not just on our beliefs, but also on the *strength* of those beliefs.**

NOTES

STEP 3
MOVING ON

This step will help students see that the strength of their convictions equals the strength with which they can resist negative peer pressure.

Option 1  Chat Room

You'll need A TV, a VCR and the video *Indiana Jones and the Last Crusade.*

Ahead of time, cue the video approximately one hour and 43 minutes from the opening graphic where the character Donovan says "The grail is mine, and you're going to get it for me." This is the six-minute scene where Donovan shoots Professor Jones and Indiana Jones goes through three tests to get the Holy Grail. The third test is the step of faith where Indy must step into open air in order to prove his belief.

Show the video clip; then discuss:

What did Donovan mean when he said, "It's time to ask yourself what you believe?" If Indy really believed the grail could heal his father, he would go after it.

Which would have been the hardest test for you to take?

Why was Indy so confident about how to face each challenge? He followed the instructions in his father's diary and trusted that his father was correct.

Explain: **Have you ever wondered what your life would be like if you had as much confidence in the instructions given in our Father's book as Indiana Jones had in his father's diary? We may say that we believe in God and what His Word says, but do we believe enough to be able to face the pressures that people put on us? Let's take a look at how you can apply what you believe to specific peer pressure situations.**

Option 2  Real Life

You'll need This book!

Share the following case study:

> Andrea's best friend, Amber, is usually a pretty good student, but lately she's having some problems getting her homework done because her parents have been fighting so much. Last night Amber didn't study at all for the big math test today. In fact, she spent the whole night crying with her head buried under her pillow, trying not to hear her dad beating on her mom.
>
> As Andrea and Amber enter their first period math class, Amber asks Andrea to let her copy off her test paper just this once. Andrea knows that Amber's a good student and she knows how hard Amber's had it lately, but she's really torn. She wants to help her friend, but she knows cheating is wrong. She finally decides that it's OK to let Amber copy just this once.

Discuss:

Is it *ever* OK to cheat? Allow for responses.

What could Andrea have done differently? First, when she found out all that Amber was going through, she could have encouraged Amber to talk to the school counselor or another trusted adult. For the upcoming test, she could have gone with Amber to talk to the math teacher and given her support while asking the teacher for help.

What if you cheat and don't get caught? Is it OK then? No, it's equally wrong regardless of whether or not you get caught—it's the action that's wrong, not the consequences.

Are there peer pressure situations that would *not* be very hard to resist because of your beliefs? (You'll probably get a wide variety of responses here, such as, taking drugs is not an issue because of their belief that drugs are bad for their body, etc.)

What are some situations where you might be more pressured because your beliefs aren't as strong?

Explain: **We all hold strong beliefs about some issues, and we tend not to be very tempted when people pressure us to do those things. In other situations,** though, we need some help in figuring out how to live out our beliefs. Let's find out how to apply what you believe to specific peer pressure situations.

Option 3 — Tough Questions

You'll need Zipporino.

1. **Why do some people believe in something and then act like they don't?** People sometimes say they believe something, but they almost always act according to what they really believe deep down. When we sin, it's because at the time we believe that what we want is more important than what God wants. There's a saying that "values are observable behaviors." This means that what we value always comes out in our actions.

2. **Why does it really matter what I believe?** Beliefs depend on two things: 1) the sincerity (or strength) of your belief; and 2) the object of your faith. It doesn't make sense to believe in something that isn't true. It's been said that you can believe sincerely, and be sincerely wrong. In other words, people who are very sincere believers in Buddha, New Age worldviews and a host of other religions, can really believe—maybe even die for their beliefs—but still be wrong in what they believe.

3. **Can the same person believe conflicting things?** No. Yes. I think so. Psychologists call this "cognitive dissonance." When we hold conflicting beliefs, it causes stress, so people either resolve the conflict by dropping or modifying one of the beliefs or by simply choosing not to think about it anymore (in which case, they don't really believe anything anymore about that issue).

4. **Aren't true believers just religious *fanatics*?** Absolutely! But that's not a bad thing! It's OK in this world to be a sports fanatic, a music fanatic even a movie fanatic—it's OK to be crazy about a lot of things, but somehow applying the term "fanatic" to a Christian is a derogatory term. There's nothing

wrong with being a fanatic; it's just important to be a fanatic about the right things. If we are fanatics the way Jesus called us to be—by loving God and loving people—people will be impressed. Some people may make fun of us, but that will merely be another test of how strong our faith is.

STEP 4 — MOVING OUT

This step will help students identify specific areas in their lives where they can apply their beliefs to negative peer pressure situations.

Option 1 — Light the Fire

You'll need Copies of "Drawing the Line" (p. 90) and pens or pencils.

Distribute "Drawing the Line" and pens or pencils and explain: **In many peer pressure situations, we need to decide ahead of time where we will draw the line—we need to decide what our beliefs *will* and will *not* allow us to do.**

Instruct students to draw a line under the statements that best show what they believe; then put a star by the statements that best summarize what they think God would say.

If your group has a high level of trust with each other, have students share what they've underlined; otherwise, let them keep their answers to themselves. In any case, encourage them to keep their handouts and to look at them during the week to remind themselves of where they are drawing the line in their lives.

Suggestion: Since this session is about convictions and beliefs, use this opportunity to share the message of the gospel. Invite anyone who hasn't already done so to invite Jesus into their lives as Lord and Savior right now!

Close in prayer, thanking God for His tremendous love for every one of His children and asking Him to help students stand firm in their beliefs in the coming weeks.

Youth Leader Tip

Option 2 Fired Up

You'll need One copy of "Moral Dilemmas" (p. 91).

Ahead of time, cut the handout into four separate dilemmas.

Explain: **We all face situations in our lives where our beliefs will be challenged and we won't know what to do. These moral dilemmas sometimes come in the form of negative peer pressure where a bunch of people are pressuring us to do something questionable. If we really know who we are and what we believe when we face these situations, we should know what to do.**

Divide students into four groups and distribute one moral dilemma to each group. Instruct groups to come up with some advice for the person in their assigned situation. Allow a few minutes for discussion; then regroup and discuss what each group came up with. If you have time, probe into what the person in each situation would gain—or lose—by following the groups' recommendations.

Close in prayer, thanking God for His tremendous love for every one of His children and asking Him to help students stand firm in their beliefs in the coming weeks.

Option 3 Spread the Fire

You'll need Just this here book.

Explain that one of the worst peer pressure situations any American teenager has faced was demonstrated on April 20, 1999, at Columbine High School in Colorado. When the killers asked if she believed in God, Cassie Bernall said yes—and was killed. Share the following excerpts from *She Said Yes: The Unlikely Martyrdom of Cassie Bernall*[1]:

> **Cassie stood up for what she believed. It is enough to know that at an age when image means everything, she was not ashamed to make a stand or afraid to say what she thought. . . .**
>
> **Cassie wasn't especially outgoing by nature, and I can't imagine how difficult it must have been for her to make herself vulnerable in this way. But she was determined to hold firm to what she knew was right, and willing to grapple with her fears and insecurities. And in the end, even if she never completely overcame these things, her assurance of who she was and what she stood for was so strong that no one could take it away from her.**

Explain: **Because this young girl stood up for what she believed, hundreds of people have been impacted by her example and become followers of Jesus Christ. When non-Christian people see the strength of your beliefs in the face of persecution and pressure, they definitely sit up and take notice—and it doesn't have to be in such drastic circumstances as Cassie faced.**

Remind students of the story of Paul and Silas in jail and how their faith and convictions impressed the jailer so much that he asked how he could be saved—and how he and his whole family were baptized by Paul and Silas that *very day* (see Acts 16:30-34)!

Divide students into small prayer groups of three to five and instruct group members to share one situation where they may face peer pressure and want to stand up for what they believe. Have each group close in prayer for the strengthening of their faith and the courage to stand up for what they believe *no matter what*.

Note
1. Permission granted to reprint excerpts from *She Said Yes* by Misty Bernall (Farmington, PA: Plough Publishing House, 1999).

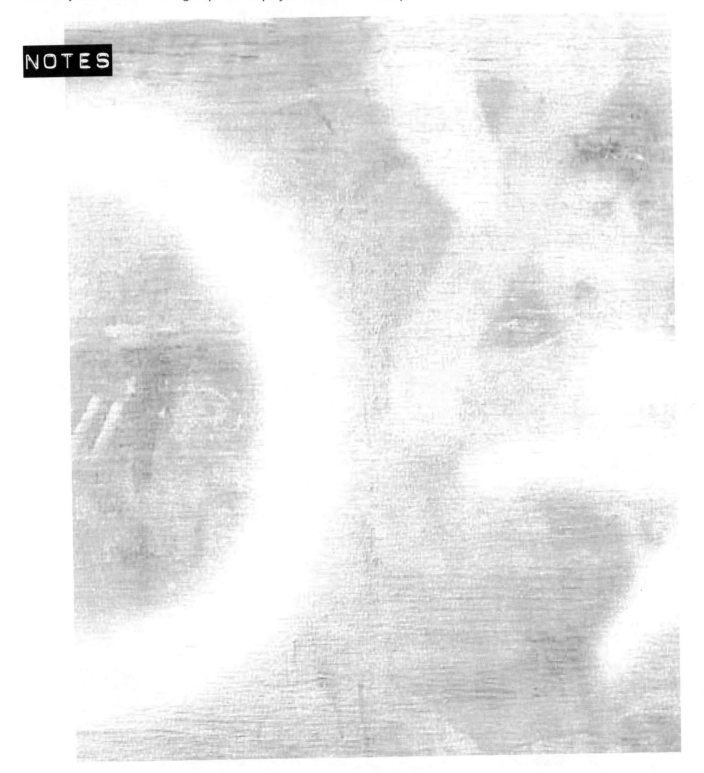

NOTES

Drawing the Line

Underline a statement in each category that best represents what you believe. Draw a star next to a statement in each category that best represents what you think God would say.

Premarital Sex

When dating someone . . .

You should never touch each other.

It's OK to hold hands.

It's OK to kiss.

It's OK to kiss deeply.

It's OK to pet.

It's OK to have sexual intercourse.

Drinking

It's never OK to drink.

It's OK to drink only if you are of legal age.

It's OK for minors to drink if your parents give it to you.

It's OK to drink at any age.

Movies

While still in junior high . . .

It's OK to go to G-rated movies.

It's OK to go to PG movies.

It's OK to go to PG-13 movies.

It's OK to go to R-rated movies with your parents' permission.

It's OK to go to R-rated movies without your parents' permission.

It's OK to go to NC-17 movies.

Lying

It's never OK to lie.

It's OK to tell little white lies.

It's OK to lie if the truth will hurt someone's feelings.

It's OK to lie if you are helping a friend.

It's OK to lie if it gets you out of trouble.

It's OK to lie for any reason.

Moral Dilemmas

Dilemma One

A man borrows his neighbor's hunting rifle, promising to return it if his neighbor wants to use it. One day the neighbor, in a fit of rage, asks for the gun—apparently with the intention to kill someone.

The man is faced with a dilemma: He can keep his promise and take a chance on being an accessory to a murder *or* he can break his promise and possibly save the neighbor from doing something he might regret. What should the man do?

Dilemma Two

Ben has just started dating Kristen. One night, Ben goes to Kristen's house to pick her up for a dance. When she comes downstairs, she spins around and asks "what do you think of my new outfit?" Ben thinks the outfit is really ugly. What should he say?

Dilemma Three

Brittany went over to Amy's house to watch a video. Even though her parents told her they didn't want her watching R-rated movies, Brittany watched the one Amy's brother rented anyway. When she got home, her parents asked her what movie they watched. What should she say?

Dilemma Four

Michael's at an amusement park with his friends and loses his wallet and all of his money. His friends don't have enough money to lend him any for lunch. While waiting in line for a ride, Michael sees a wallet on the ground. He picks it up and sees that it has $30 in it, but no identification. What should he do?

Devotions in Motion

WEEK SIX: YOU'VE GOT TO STAND FFOR SOMETHING OR YOU'LL FALL FOR ANYTHING

DAY 1

FAST FACTS

Wander over to Ephesians 1:3,4.

God Says

Who do you think you are?

My friends tell me I am the prettiest girl they know," one eighth grader says.

"I am a student," says another.

"I am John and Judy's son" or "I am a crocodile hunter," two others might say.

Sometimes the way we see ourselves depends on things that we do (in the case of the crocodile hunter) or the people we are related to (in the case of John and Judy's son) or even what others say about us (in the case of the eighth-grade beauty queen). But with all of the things we believe about ourselves and with all of the things that others tell us about ourselves, do we hear what God says about who we are? Who does God think you are?

I Do

Read Ephesians 1:3,4 out loud. In every place in the passage that has the words "us" or "we," put your name instead. Write out parts of the passage or the whole thing with your name to remind you of who you are!

Ok, given what you've just read in Ephesians, what two things should be different about your day? Pray that God will help those two things happen!

FOLD HERE --

DAY 4

QUICK QUESTIONS

Philippians 2:1-4

God Says

Kevin couldn't believe what was happening to him The least popular girl in the whole school, Melissa, got paired up with him for a huge science project. That meant Kevin would have to be working with Melissa every day for 53 minutes for the next six weeks. The rest of Kevin's friends ended up with cool partners, but Kevin ended up with the only girl in the whole class who wore the same outfit all week and only washed her hair every two weeks.

If Kevin wanted to practice Philippians 2:1-4 in his science class, what would he do?

☐ Rig an experiment so that it throws goo all over her and then join the rest of the class in laughing at her.

☐ Get to know Melissa and find at least one thing he can appreciate about her.

☐ Pretend to be sick, so he'd spend more time in the nurse's office than in science.

I Do

Kevin's in a tough place—torn between what everybody else will think and Melissa's feelings. But imagine how different your school would be if everybody else treated others as more important than themselves.

Name one person in your school who often gets made fun of. What can you do this week to show that you consider that person better than yourself?

DAY 2

FAST FACTS
Turn To 1 Peter 2:9,10.

God Says

You run out onto the playground. Your heart pounds and your feet sweat. Bill and Ted are the two team captains, and they start calling names out for the kickball game. Will you be chosen?

Each of us knows the feeling of being chosen or being left out of a game or event. The good news is that God has already chosen each of us, and nobody is left out unless they choose to not respond to God's choice of them.

I Do.

After you are chosen to be a part of a team, what are some of the responsibilities of being a part of that team?

Being chosen by God is kind of like being on a team. What is one big responsibility that you can take on and do this week as a part of God's team?

FOLD HERE -

DAY 3

QUICK QUESTIONS
Go back to familiar territory and find 1 Peter 2:11.

God Says

Aliens are little greenish people with weird-looking faces who come to other planets to abduct humans for painful and gross experiments back on their own planets, right? Well, according to the verse you just read, aliens are actually a lot more like us than we think.

According to this passage, who are aliens?

I Do.

What a weird thought, huh? People who follow Jesus (that's you and I) are aliens and strangers in this world? The point is that we are different from regular earthlings because we follow Jesus.

Think of three ways that you are an alien (or three ways that you are different from the people around you because you follow Jesus).

What are two other things you feel you ought to do differently to be more like an alien in this world because you follow Jesus? Now go do those two things!

© 2001 Gospel Light. Permission to photocopy granted. *Peer Pressure*

On the Move

100 PERCENT PURE

As a seventh grader walking to the school cafeteria, I couldn't believe my eyes. On the fence near the gym, there hung a new brightly painted banner:

COME TRY OUR NEW CAFETERIA HAMBURGERS. NOW 100% BEEF.

I kid you not. That's what it said.

That started all sorts of rumors. If the burgers were now 100 percent beef, what had they been made of before? Vegetables? Frogs? Dogs?

We didn't know, and to be honest, we didn't want to know. But let's just say I started taking my own lunch from that point on.

See, what I wanted was to know that every hamburger that had ever been made in that cafeteria was 100 percent beef. Pure beef. Nothing else added.

And that's really what it means to be pure—to be 100 percent of one thing. Being 95 percent doesn't cut it. It has to be 100 percent to be pure.

I once heard about this eighth grader, Danny, who decided to be 100 percent purely dedicated to God. He knew that this meant he had to stay away from gossip, being mean to others, pornography on the Internet and a whole bunch of other temptations.

There was one temptation that almost got the best of Danny. His friend, George, had an older brother who had had the same science teacher two years earlier. This teacher was pretty lazy, so he gave the same tests year after year. George had copies of all of his brother's tests and soon started handing them out ahead of time to his friends.

So Danny had a choice: Either accept the copy that George was offering and get an A for sure or try to take the test on his own and get a C like always.

Before I tell you what he did, what would you do? Would you accept the test, telling yourself every-body else is doing it—besides what's the big deal about a test? or would you remain 100 percent dedicated to God and do the right thing?

Well, Danny decided to take the test on his own, and get this:

He did better than anybody else on the test. Instead of just an A, he got an A-plus!

The story of Danny is a true one, but like they say in TV shows, "Some details have been changed to protect the innocent." It's actually a story from the Bible. Daniel 1 to be exact. There was no science test that Danny (a.k.a. Daniel) faced, but instead, he had to choose whether he would defile himself by eating the royal food and wine, which although tasty, had been partially offered to idols. Daniel could have said to himself, It's no big deal. It's only a little meal here and there, and my, don't those steaks look scrumptous. Instead, he remained pure, eating vegetables and drinking water. At the end of 10 days, Daniel actually looked healthier and better nourished than the young men who ate the royal food.

There are a few lessons we learn from the story of Daniel. And if you want to remain pure in a world that is tempting you with hatred, violence, sex, alcohol, drugs and pretty much every sin that you can imagine, you might want to pay attention to them.

Little Choices Matter

A meal here, a meal there; a science test here, a science test there. They all seem like they're no-big-deal, but every time you make a wrong choice, you become less than 100 percent set apart for God.

Imagine your life is a circle like a hamburger patty (or if you're more in the mood for dessert, a pie). What percent of the circle is dedicated to God? Be honest now. What percent of the circle is dedicated to doing what you want to? What percent is dedicated to doing what others want you to do? The little choices you make along the way are like pieces out of that circle that make it less and less dedicated to God.

Flee Temptation

My hunch is that Daniel didn't stick around the kitchen when the royal food was being prepared, smelling it and wishing he could have some. That would only make it harder for him to say no when the time came.

The same is true for us today. If you figure out that something is tempting you and may make you less than 100 percent pure, get away from it. Run. Flee. Skeedaddle out of there. Remember the vivid picture painted in Proverbs 26:11: "As a dog returns to its vomit, so a fool repeats his folly." Gross.

Join Forces

If you read Daniel 1, you'll see that Daniel wasn't alone in making the choice to be 100 percent dedicated to God. He had three friends with him: Shadrach, Meshach and Abednego (of fiery furnace fame). All four of the friends refused to eat the unholy food and all four were served the same simple meals. I'll bet it gave Daniel a bunch of comfort and courage when he looked over and saw Shadrach and Abednego eating the same broccoli and carrots that he was.

Hook up with other Christians on your campus or keep in close touch with friends from church when you're making those tough decisions. There's power in numbers—especially since one of those on your side is God!